Tr

Trade Winds

Absolute Press

Dedication

Firstly to Ivan, my husband, the dearest man in the world, who has so enriched my life; and to all the people in the West Indies who received me with such warmth and hospitality.

Acknowledgements

Firstly to Paula Borton for her consistently kind and patient help to me. I must also thank Vicky Hayward, who had the foresight and enthusiasm when the idea was in its earliest stages, to encourage me tirelessly – without her the book would probably not have developed. The British Library. The Bristol Archives. Bristol City Museum and Art Gallery. Tate & Lyle. The Royal Commonwealth Society. West India Committee. Institute of Commonwealth Studies. Jamaica High Commission. Grenada High Commission. City of Bristol Record Office – the map reproduced on page 10 is the property of Bristol City Council, ref 38032.

Published by Absolute Press
Scarborough House, 29 James St West, Bath.

First published November 1987
This paperback edition published November 1996

© Cristine MacKie, 1987 and 1996

Printed in Great Britain by The Longdunn Press Limited,
Barton Manor, St Philips, Bristol.

Contents

Conversion Tables

All these conversions are approximate. They have either been rounded up or down. Never mix metric and imperial measures in one recipe; stick to one system or the other.

Weights

½oz	10g
1oz	25g
1½oz	40g
2oz	50g
3oz	75g
4oz	110g
5oz	150g
6oz	175g
7oz	200g
8oz	225g
9oz	250g
10oz	275g
12oz	350g
13oz	375g
14oz	400g
15oz	425g
1lb	450g
1¼lb	550g
1½lb	700g
2lb	900g
3lb	1.4kg
4lb	1.8kg
5lb	2.3kg

Measurements

¼ inch	0.5cm
½ inch	1cm
1 inch	2.5cm
2 inch	5cm
3 inch	7.5cm
4 inch	10cm
6 inch	15cm
7 inch	18cm
8 inch	20.5cm
9 inch	23cm
11 inch	28cm
12 inch	30.5cm

Oven Temperatures

Mark 1	275°F	140°C
Mark 2	300°F	150°C
Mark 3	325°F	170°C
Mark 4	350°F	180°C
Mark 5	375°F	190°C
Mark 6	400°F	200°C
Mark 7	425°F	220°C
Mark 8	450°F	230°C
Mark 9	475°F	240°C

Volume

1 fl oz	25ml
2 fl oz	50ml
3 fl oz	75ml
5 (¼ pint)	150ml
10 (½ pint)	275ml
15 (¾ pint)	400ml
1 pint	570ml
1¼ pint	700ml
1½ pint	900ml
1¾ pint	1 litre
2 pint	1.1 litre
2¼ pint	1.3 litre
2½ pint	1.4 litre
2¾ pint	1.6 litre
3 pint	1.75 litre
3¼ pint	1.8 litre
3½ pint	2 litre
3¾ pint	2.1 litre
4 pint	2.3 litre
5 pint	2.8 litre
6 pint	3.4 litre
7 pint	4.0 litre
8 (1 gal)	4.5 litre

Volume Imperial/American

¼ pint	⅔ cup
½ pint	1¼ cups
¾ pint	2 cups
1 pint	2½ cups
1½ pints	3¾ cups
2 pints	5 cups

Calorie Sheet

Vegetables
(per hundred grams)

Achee 30
Artichoke 29
Aubergine 27
Beans
    Lima 146
    Bodi or Yard 34
    Soya 398
    String 35
    Pigeon 118
Beetroot 44
Breadfruit 81
Cassava 132
Châtaigne
    (Chestnut) 194
Christophene 31
Corn 129
Cowpeas (dried) . . 341
Dasheen 92
Eddoe 92
Kohl Rabi 31
Ochra
    (Ladies fingers)
    or Brindis 42
Patechoi
    (Chinese cabbage) 26
Peppers 38
Plantain 122

Pumpkin 30
Spinach 19
Sweet potato 166
Swiss chard 27
Tannia 132
Yam 100

Fruit
(per hundred grams)

Avocado 30
Banana 94
Barbados cherry . . . 36
Carambola 36
Cashew fruit 46
Coconut
    mature 296
    immature 122
    milk 18
Golden apple 95
Governor plum . . . 108
Grenadilla 20
Hog plum 70
Lemon 29
Lime 32
Mammee apple 47
Mango common . . . 59
Orange
    sweet 42
    sour 50

Pawpaw or Papaya . 28
Pineapple 52
Pomerac 51
Sapodilla 94
Saddock (grapefruit) 34
Samsop 60
Sorrel 55
Surinam cherry 51
Tamarind 272

Introduction

What is Caribbean cooking? To travellers with a sense of nostalgia and those who have only visited the islands in their imagination I hope this book will kindle and inspire the senses. Caribbean cooking is a mood, a sense of well being, time allowed. A world where glinting green spears of palm fronds rattle at the jalousies as Mynah birds shriek cries of encouragement outside the window. Where, as the early morning sun climbs overhead, the light becomes incandescent and the colours luminous. The Caribbean sea is the backcloth, its horizon, hard edged, with a violet line deepening to royal blue. As the ocean swells towards the land its waters become crystal clear, marbled with emerald where the waves wash gently over the coral and still themselves on the bleached white sand. As noon approaches, enticing smells are carried from distant kitchens on the trade winds, mingling with the perfumed scent of frangipani – perhaps the tantalising aroma of rice and peas simmering in freshly squeezed coconut milk seasoned with a piece of pig's tail, or the unforgettable smell of meat searing in oil and burnt sugar, tinged with the subtle spiciness of freshly grated nutmeg, thyme and spring onions.

I have deliberately chosen recipes that capture the feel and flavour of the Caribbean; recipes that emphasise the importance of personal imagination and improvisation. They have been set against the fascinating background of life in the British West Indies since the early seventeenth century, taking the reader into the great houses and the slave quarters, drawing extensively on original sources – travellers' journals, household accounts and recipe books of the nabob families – to explain how this tradition of cooking grew up against a background of the sugar and rum trades.

Travellers of today may find it hard to imagine that a good many of the most characteristic of Caribbean recipes evolved from the great period of English cooking and were introduced by the planters in the sixteenth and seventeenth centuries. These dishes were, of course, adapted to the produce and particular tastes of the West Indies. Many have become unrecognisable by their absorption of Spanish, French and Dutch influences, while others have been passed on from one generation to the next and have remained virtually unchanged, thus preserving many dishes that have been lost to English cooking. Even in the eighteenth century the frequency of trade across the Atlantic was such that exotic West Indian produce appeared regularly on the tavern menus of the great British sugar ports. Today the pattern of migration is reversed and virtually all the ingredients you will need to recreate these wonderful dishes are readily available in good markets and specialist stores, both here and in North America.

I was once asked the question, did I not feel that because I was living in two societies, that I was culturally and emotionally uncommitted? I was so stunned by apparent lack of insight that I was forced to ponder long and deep. Although the idea for this book had already taken hold, suddenly I saw a greater need for its existence than ever before. Through my long indulgences in these glorious and sometimes extraordinary experiences, I had been fortunate to become part of two contrasting worlds. There was no division. On the contrary it was all perceived with the same eyes and imagination. The realisation gave me a sense of exultance. Today in our world of multi-cultures it is more important than ever before that our societies learn to see the differences as an enrichment of the world we all live in, not a separating force.

As a child, the world that I inhabited was the world of the imagination, one that naturally I had never seen. When I first travelled to Jamaica as an adult, it was to meet with a staggering beauty and intensity of experience that I was ready for. I could only look and look and truly possess it. So fabulous were these extremes of experience in these contrasting worlds of mine, that I hope to share some of the delights and satisfactions through the recipes and travellers' tales in this book.

Longitude West from London

LABRADOR

NEWFOUNDLAND

A Plain Chart of

THE TRACK
of the Ship
LLOYD
from Bristol to Dominica
& from thence to LONDON

Belle isle
C. Race
Grand Banks
False Bank

THE

WESTERN OCEAN.

Western
Islands

Covvo
Flores
Fyal   Pico   Gratiosa
Tercera
St. George   St. Michael
St. Mary

Bermudas

TROPIC of CANCER.

Eluthera   Bahama Islands
Cat I.   Watling I.
Exuma   Long I.
Crooked I.
Mayaguana
Caicos Bank
Inagua   Turks
Cuba   Salt Key   Abrolhos
Gallega   Anegada
C. Cicaron
Hispaniola
C. Tiberon

Porto Rico
St. Cruz
Sombrero
Anguilla
St. Martin
St. Barthol
Saba   St. Christopher
Nevis   Barbuda
Antego   Deseada
Mariegalante
Guadaloupe
Domingo
Martinico
St. Lucia   ISLANDS
St. Vincent   Barbadoes
Granada   Tobago

CARIBBEE

C. Conquest
C. de Vela
La Hacha

BAY
of
BISCAY

S. GEORGE'S
Channel

LISBON

Straits

Gibraltar

FEZ

MOROCCO
&
BARARY

CANARY
Palma
Ferro   Gomera
Teneriffe
Grand Canary
Lancerota
Forteventura

ISLANDS

Guahetan

AFRICA

Arguin

CAPE DE VERD
St. Antonio   St. Vincent   St. Lucia
St. Nicholas   O. Sal
St. Jago   Bonavista
Brava   Mayo

ISLANDS

Senegal

GAMBIA

R. Gambia

Shoals of

Madeira
Porto Santo

Trade Winds Outward 1773

N. Pocock 1771

A Short History of the West Indies

In 1595, Sir Walter Raleigh began his raids on Trinidad and South America. They ended with an inexplicable return to England in 1617 and imprisonment in the Tower of London. It was then that he wrote *The Discovery of the Large and Beautiful Empire of Guiana*. The book was published some months after the event. It is a fascinating account of the excursion. In Raleigh's own words, 'I made them understand,' he wrote after landing in Trinidad in 1595 for the first time, 'that I was a servant of the Queen who was the great Casique (Lord) of the North, and a virgine, and had more Casique under her than there were trees in that island.' He continued to address the Indian chiefs through his interpreter, 'that she Elizabeth was an enemy to the Castellani, in respect of their tyranny and oppression and that she delivered all such nations as were about her, as were by them oppressed and having freed all the coast of the Northern world from their servitude, had sent me to free them also and with all to defend the country of Guiana from their invasion and conquest.' The Indians were undoubtedly delighted at this prospect of release from the Spanish oppression and were full of admiration when shown portraits of Elizabeth, Queen of England.

The Spanish had first arrived in the late fifteenth century when Christopher Columbus made his first landfall in the Bahamas, steadfastly believing, and did so until his dying day, that he had found the islands lying off the coast of Eastern Asia, which would prove easy stepping stones to India. The name West Indies remains a testimony to this belief.

The West Indies formed a gateway to the founding of a great empire in Central and South America.

Domingo da Vera, returning from an expedition, wrote of 'a high city with its temples full of gold . . . of clothed and civilized people . . . there were so many Indians as would shadowe the sun, and so much gold as all yonder plaine will not contain it . . . .'

The Spanish foothold in the Caribbean remained unchallenged until the mid-seventeenth century, when tales of the riches of the new Spanish empire reached Europe invoking interest and envy, and the struggle for the new empire began.

Despite the Spanish grip on the islands it did not prevent British ships travelling to those waters and even landing in Trinidad. In 1595 on the 31st January, while Raleigh was still waiting his first commission, Robert Dudley arrived at the island of Trinidad and may well have given the very first account of a trans-Atlantic voyage. It was recorded on Christmas day, ' . . . a very hot day, the men swimming from ship to ship to make greate cheere to each other ... the flying fish rising from the sea like a flock of frightened larkes'. It was perhaps the elation caused by the illusory prospect of finding gold that caused Dudley to appropriate the island of Trinidad for the English crown, by the simple device of affixing a leaden plate to a tree near the supposed gold mines. It bore the Queen of England's arms and a Latin inscription. He also observed that the Indians came on board and gave him, 'hennes, hogs, plantains, potatoes, pinos (pineapples) and tobacco ... the country is fertile and full of fruits, strange beasts and fowle ... ' Francis Drake, perhaps the most famous and capable seaman of his time, also embarked on fearsome and well executed forays into Spanish territory. *El Draque* became a name to strike fear into the hearts of the Spanish settlers.

Understandably, the Spanish would not allow any interlopers, whether it was in the order of formal trading, or the nefarious activities of the buccaneers. Wrangles over trade and territory between the Spanish and other would be colonists, namely the English and French became a long standing feature of the West Indies.

The new colonies of Carolina and Virginia on the Eastern seaboard of America were developing rapidly and undermined the tobacco trade in Trinidad. The Dutch threatened to colonise the island until the English and French combined to destroy them. The province was proving to be a liability to Spain, but its strategic position to the Orinoco (gateway to the gold of El Dorado) made them fearful to withdraw, as they were doing in the other islands north of Trinidad. Reports to the King of Spain wrote ceaselessly of requests for more men, money and ships. There were complaints of neglect, ruin and contraband. The waters around the islands were no longer the 'Spanish Sea'.

The Governor of Trinidad wrote to the King of Spain, 'I am sick in bed, and am surrounded by the enemy' (that was the English) 'and hostile natives. I have asked four times for help. I don't believe any one in the world has to put up with such hard luck or such labours.' He went on, 'tell them in Santa Fe that the church is more a doorway than a church ... we have nothing to celebrate mass with and our Friars are as a result disconsolate ... our bodies show through our rags and the dead are buried without shrouds.'

The above account gives an idea of the desperate situation and difficulties that confronted the men from Europe who lived there long before the more recent and familiar history of the sugar plantations and subsequently unpleasant facts of the slave trade that sprang up to support its industry.

The extraordinary fact was, that the Spanish would not plant crops to survive, and the Indians would not work for them anyway (although they were taken as slaves). Smallpox broke out and the inhabitants took to the bushes and scratched an existence from the soil and lived as the Indians had done before them. Governors came and went from Spain, finding the town, 'over grown with woods and thickets, the citizens living in the bush with the negros as their companions'.

As the dreams of El Dorado faded, Trinidad was no longer valuable. The Dutch, now a sea trading nation of some worth, became a major protagonist in the West Indian theatre. Their West India Company offered the most serious challenge to Spanish pre-eminence in the Caribbean. The

Dutch, however, were not interested in colonising but in commerce and trade and every blow they dealt Spain were opportunities in the 1620's for the English and French to settle in the outer islands such as St. Kitts and Barbados. The new areas of settlement in the Caribbean coincided with the great flood of immigration from England, where there were more men than jobs or land.

A traveller of that time, Richard Ligon, lost his fortune in foreign speculation and journeyed to Barbados in 1647. On his return to England he was sent to the debtors' prison at Newgate and wrote *A True and Exact History of the Island of Barbados.* He described his fellow female outward bound travellers as well able to fend for themselves, 'The major part of them having been taken from Bridewell, Turnbole Street and such like places of education'. A soldier who also travelled out there with Venable Penn's expedition observed, 'the island of Barbados is inhabited by all sorts, with the English, French, Dutch, Scotes, Irish, Spaniards, they being the Jues, with igones and misarabell Negors borne to perpetual slavery thay and thaer seed ... this land is the dung hill whar our England doth cast forth it's rubbish.' Most of them were from the West Country, and Royalist in sympathy, while Jamaica attracted the Republicans. Rich and poor left alike with the approaching civil war.

In 1653, Jamaica was also won from the Spanish, the new settlers engaged in a pastoral existence growing maize, tobacco and cotton, which at that time was of primary importance.

When the tobacco and cotton trades were eventually undermined by similar crops grown in the North American colonies, it was the Dutch who introduced the idea and technique of growing sugar to the French and English islands. As the main trader of the West Indies it was to their advantage to encourage any crop which could be sold in Europe. The growth of sugar production radically changed the agricultural and social foundations of the islands. Sugar production and its requirement of a large intensive work force resulted in the burgeoning of the infamous slave trade and the formation of the triangular voyage. Ships sailed from England to Africa with trade goods such as guns and beads and exchanged their cargo for African slaves to run what was known as the Middle Passage to the West Indies, where their human cargo was sold to the plantations. They returned to England with the raw product that was refined into sugar. Never before in history had there been the enslavement of so many for the enrichment of so few.

Despite the numerous wars with the French and Spanish, the British West Indies reached the zenith of their prosperity at the end of the seventeenth century, the islands supplying 9 per cent of English imports as against 8 per cent from the mainland colonies. By the mid-eighteenth century the golden age of sugar was past, the French having taken over from the British in this sphere, and many of the islands turned to the production of crops such as cocoa, coffee, ginger and nutmeg. Despite these efforts the interest of the mother country in her West Indian colonies was slowly waning to the great dismay of the planters. It was increasingly obvious how dependent the islands were on the colonial links, trade was their lifeline and the navy afforded them a much needed protection. The West Indies were also acutely feeling the reverberation of political upheaval in Europe. In France there was revolution.

Victor Hugues, Robespierre's emissary, arrived in the island of Guadaloupe with a force of 1500 men and seized it from the British, executed 300 French Royalists and proclaimed the end of slavery. In Haiti another Negro leader, Toussaint, rebelled and joined the French Republic. Jamaica also underwent revolts by runaway slaves. In Trinidad, Governor Chacon almost lost control. Although Spain and France had signed a peace treaty and the waters between Trinidad and the South American coast were neutral, they were used by all and sundry and with no regard to the fact that the island was still in Spanish hands. French privateers haunted those waters and the British were constantly trying to rout them out. By 1801, the ensuing war between England and Napoleon contributed even more to the general turbulence in the area which eventually ceased with the Treaty of Amiens, which left Trinidad in British hands. Thus ended three hundred years of Spanish rule and the death of any dreams of what might have been. The West Indies were now firmly in the commercial grip of Britain and North America.

The ideas of liberty, equality and the notion of the 'noble savage' espoused by Rousseau and his revolutionary followers added credence to the anti-slavery lobby in England. William Wilberforce spear-headed the movement and eloquently rallied support; his success was such that the Act for the abolition of the slave trade came in force in 1808. The consequence of this Act for the West Indies was far reaching and the planters desperately carried on the slave trade illicitly until the Emancipation Act of 1833. Thomas Carlyle wrote in 1849 that emancipation had ruined the West Indies and encouraged slaves to idleness, lying in the sun and eating pumpkin and yam. Anthony Trollope writing a little later in 1860 would have us believe that not only had emancipation ruined the islands, but that the great house of European plantocracy was the centre of culture and elegance in the West Indies and the only path to civilisation.

In 1810, Lord Liverpool sent a dispatch to the Governor of Trinidad, which gives us an insight into the British government's attitude to Trinidad which was very different to that of Jamaica and Barbados. 'It so happens, that the circumstances of the island of Trinidad are in many respects so materially different from those of all the West India colonies, that supporting the system of government established in those islands is to be the best that could be afforded to them in their situation. It would not follow that the same system could be rendered applicable, either in justice or policy to the island of Trinidad . . . in most of the West India islands, except Dominica the great body of proprietors and white inhabitants are British, or the descendants of British families, to whom the British Constitution and the laws have become familiar . . . but in the island of Trinidad, the white population consists of a mixture of all nations. The greater part of them wholly ignorant of the British Constitution.' The question then arose of what sort of government the now British West Indian island of Trinidad might enjoy. In Jamaica, the traditional pattern of an imitation British Constitution was already set. That being a legislative house of two chambers; the lower one, elected with a governor, representing the sovereign, cooperated with an elected representative of the people. It was decided to make Trinidad a Crown Colony, with essential powers reserved to the government at home.

The collapse of the slave trade, radically transformed West Indian society giving rise to the growth of free villages, a peasant population, the crumbling of the plantation system and the encouragement of immigration. In the nineteenth century the development of Trinidad flowered and its small population grew. It suffered, however, from an acute shortage of labour and the planters clamoured for the encouragement of immigrant labour. Lord Elgin, the Governor of Jamaica rejected this attitude, deploring their reliance on immigration to circumvent the need to come to terms with the already existing freed slaves and to, 'retard the growth of that more intimate sympathy between the enlightened friends of the planter and the peasant I am so desirous to promote.'

Many immigrants were recruited from Portugal, but the effects of the climate and conditions were quite appalling. They petitioned, 'men and women and children have suffered the greatest misery and oppression on the several estates, where they have been forced to work beyond their strength by coercion of the whip with out proper shelter at night or adequate food by day ... the consolation of religion has been denied them in sickness and death.'

Immigration was contemplated from all sources, even from Sierra Leone. Despite the Treaty of Amiens and the Congress of Vienna agreements to abolish slavery, the Cuban and Brazilian slave ships continued in direct contravention. British ships made good use of this, regularly bedevilling their relations with France, Spain and the U.S.A. by insisting on their right to search the ships, they would then seize the cargo of African slaves and add them to the new labour forces in the islands. The problem was not solved until the planters recruited manpower from India in 1844 when the first ship arrived in Trinidad from Calcutta. By 1883, the East Indians formed about a third of the total population and were largely responsible for the great increase in the production of rice and their skill in irrigation methods was a contributory factor to the expansion of sugar production in Trinidad. However,

by the early part of the twentieth century most of the Indian population were off the estates living in scattered settlements as small cultivators.

By the beginning of the twentieth century it is possible to see the growing influence of the United States in West Indian affairs. European domination was becoming a thing of the past.

It may seem a digression to mention a border dispute between British Guiana and Venezuela at this point, except remote as it may seem to us it brought sharply into focus the United States as a bright new star in the Caribbean firmament. Venezuela had repeatedly pressed the United States for support in its claims. The United States made three vital points that have influenced their foreign policy to this very day. The then Secretary of State said, 'today the United States is practically sovereign on the continent (that is the South American continent) and its fiat is law upon the subjects to which it confines its interposition'. Secondly, 'the sheer physical distance that separates Europe from America, makes any permanent union between Europe and the United States unnaturel and inexpedient'. Thirdly, 'the U.S. government has been interested in the whole area of Latin America and is very concerned that the new nations do not fall into the control of the European powers'. This outlook led to the famous Monroe Doctrine. Lord Salisbury replied most strongly that Britain's relations with her colonies were 'not unnatural or inexpedient'. Times were changing however; by 1898, the U.S.A. had achieved industrial supremacy and supplanted Great Britain. Even as far back as 1835, Richard Cobden who had led British nineteenth century capitalism said about America, 'here will one day centre the civilization, the wealth, the power of the entire world.' In 1899 the *Washington Post* wrote, 'the taste of empire is in the mouth of the people, even as the taste of blood is in the jungle'.

The balance of power had swung so dramatically by the time Theodore Roosevelt was in office he said, 'I should my self like to shape our foreign policy with a purpose of ultimately driving off this continent every foreign power. I would begin with Spain and in the end would take every other nation including England'.

Europe was becoming increasingly more consumed by affairs at home. Anglo-French rivalry over Egypt brought them to the brink of war. France had allied with Russia, while Britain disputed with Russia over Afghanistan, Tibet and Persia. The Kaiser was building the most powerful navy ever. Europe no longer looked to its old interests in the Caribbean.

As a result of the Spanish-American conflict the Americans acquired their first colony in the Caribbean and so followed the tradition set by the Europeans. Roosevelt wrote ' . . . you must prevent any talk of peace (with Spain) until we get Puerto Rico, the Phillipines as well as securing the independence of Cuba'.

The Spanish Empire, once sanctioned by Papal dispensation in 1493, no longer existed. In 1904 the Assistant Secretary of State said, 'no picture of our future exists which does not contemplate and comprehend the United States as the dominant power in the Caribbean Sea'.

By the 1930s, however, the West Indies, although a disparate population, had formed a national identity resulting in a campaign for political reform. Up to 1944 the majority of people in the British West Indies had no vote; only then did the colonial office announce a policy leading towards self-government for the West Indies. In the 1960s Jamaica, Trinidad and Tobago moved towards independence, whilst it was agreed that Antigua with Berbuda and Redonda, St. Kitts, Nevis, Anguilla, Dominica, Grenada, St. Lucia and St. Vincent would become an Associated State.

We have seen through the writings and journals a glimpse of what the reality of being there in 1595 onwards was really like. The goal of El Dorado proved only to be a grand illusion both for the Conquistador and Raleigh. The venture only produced an unprofitable and unwieldy fragment of the Spanish Empire, where the indigenous Indian was destroyed only to be replaced by the African black. From 1797 onwards the islands were exploited for sugar, resulting in complex consequences for the slave holder, slaves, reactionaries and radicals alike.

The Caribbean is a part of the world where all has been taken with little returned. I believe it to be important that visitors to these beautiful islands should take with them some insight into the history and background of its peoples. To enjoy the wonderful countryside, the sea and food, but with an understanding of what has gone before.

Glossary

Ackee, Achee, Akee This extremely attractive tree was brought from West Africa by Captain Bligh of the notorious *Bounty*. It produces scarlet fruit which when ripe splits open revealing a yellow brain-like substance. Its delicate flavour is reminiscent of scrambled eggs.

Arrowroot An underground rhizome from which comes the starchy white powder and is used as a thickening agent in sauces and stews. It is far less oppressive than flour or corn starch.

Aubergine also known as **Garden Egg, Melongene, Belangere, Brinjal, Eggplant**

Avocado also known as **Zaboca, Alligator Pear** or even **Midshipman's Butter**.

Banana There are over one hundred cultivated varieties of this seedless fruit we know so well, (the wild varieties do have seeds). The fruit originated in east Asia and was observed by Alexander the Great on his travels to India. They were brought to the Canary Islands by the Portuguese soon after 1400 and then imported to the West Indies. They are rich in vitamin C, and low in protein and fat, while high in carbohydrates and potassium. When buying ripe bananas, or even the unripened ones, be sure to choose unblemished fruit. Like the sweet potato the fruit darkens very quickly when exposed to air; to prevent discoloration try dipping the peeled fruit into fresh lime or lemon juice, and only cut with a stainless steel knife.

Here are some varieties found in the West Indies:

Gros Michel, Lacatan and Governor The first is eaten raw and the other two are cooked.

Matabooro, Man Killer, Bluggoe Figs A short variety, eaten cooked.

Morocco Plantain, Blugger, Mocco, Mafube Eaten cooked.

Plantain Now frequently seen in markets here, eaten cooked. Delicious!

Silk Eaten ripe.

Sucrier This is the smallest known variety and can be eaten cooked or raw. It has a very thick skin and although delicious the flesh is slightly tart.

The leaves of the banana tree make an excellent substitute for greaseproof paper or foil and even plates. They do add a delicate flavour to any food wrapped in them.

Beans Often called peas in many of the islands.

Black-eyed Peas These beans are white with a black 'eye'. They were first brought from West Africa and can be eaten fresh or dried.

Bodi, Bode, Cowpea, Bora When fresh they are cooked like runner beans. The pea alone is used when dried.

Red Beans, Kidney Beans In Jamaica they are used in the traditional dish *rice and peas*.

Pigeon Peas These are available both fresh and dried. If dried they should be soaked overnight before use. They are imported fresh in tins and are available from specialist shops.

Breadfruit First introduced to the West Indies from West Africa in 1792 by Captain Bligh. It is a large green fruit with a rough skin. It can be baked whole in its skin or peeled, boiled or fried like a potato.

Caimite, Caimito, Star Apple This fruit is about the size of an apple. When you cut it across you will see the seeds arranged in the shape of a star.

Callaloo, Calaloo, Calalou, Callau This is the main ingredient in what is probably the most famous of all the island soups. The soup can be made with two varieties of the same plant which are regularly interchanged. Taro is one variety which belongs to the arum family, it is also known as eddoe, baddo, coco and it is a root plant. The leaves of this are called callaloo. The alternative is the malanga, otherwise known as dasheen, tanier, yautia and tannia. The roots can be treated like potatoes and the leaves are also called callaloo. In other countries you may substitute the humble spinach.

Cashew Nuts A native tree of the tropics producing edible nuts, which may be eaten raw or roasted. The fruit can be stewed, made into jam or eaten raw, though they are rather tart.

Cassava, Manioc, Mandioca, Yucca The tuberous root is peeled, boiled and eaten as a vegetable, or made into flour. The cassava meal is known here as farine and tapioca is also a product of it. There are two kinds, one is the bitter variety which is poisonous until cooked and the other is the sweet variety.

Celery Readily available in West Indian markets. The stalks are much slimmer than the European variety and the flavour much stronger so be sparing in its use; this does indeed apply to all herbs grown in the tropics.

Châtaigne French for chestnut. The fruit from the West Indies is easily interchangeable with the European variety.

Chocho, Christophene, Coyote, Choyote This is a tropical squash, which originated from Mexico. Inside the prickly, pale green skin is one seed, that can be eaten.

Dasheen)	These are all starchy root vegetables and may be prepared as you would a potato, although the dasheen is gelatinous and so less versatile. They may all be baked, boiled and roasted. You may also eat the leaves of the eddoe and the dasheen which are called callaloo.
Yam)	
Cush cush)	
Eddoes)	

Guava Derived from the Spanish name *Guayaba*. This fruit comes from a small tropical tree from South America. It is a yellow pear-shaped fruit and is mostly made into jelly or guava cheese. They may also be eaten raw.

Mango Fruit of an evergreen tree which is native to tropical Asia although East Indian in origin. When green and unripe they may be used in savoury dishes or pickled. When ripe they can be peeled and eaten fresh or used in drinks, chutneys and desserts.

Ochra, Okra, Ladies' fingers, Bamie They were introduced to the Caribbean from West Africa but are thought to have originated from Asia. They are best prepared young and lightly boiled.

Otaheite Apple, Pomerac, Plum Rose, Molly Apple You can see this fruit growing inwardly towards the centre of the tree so shedding a marvellous red glow up and along its trunk. It is a red pear-shaped fruit which is mostly used for stewing or for jam.

Papaya, Paw Paw, Carica This fruit grows in clusters on the trunk of a small tree which is native to South America. When the fruit is green it can be used as a tenderiser for tough meat or made into chutney. When the fruit turns a good even yellow it may be eaten like melon.

Pumpkin, Calabaza The best variety is Jamaican, with its dark green skin and golden flesh. Don't attempt any of the recipes with the tasteless European variety.

Sour Sop This is the fruit of a tropical American tree. A sour sop is dark green and slightly spiny. The fruit can be peeled, seeded and the remaining pulp made into a refreshing drink.

Sweet Potato The skins can vary in colour from yellow to brown with a glorious hint of crimson. They may be peeled and prepared as you would a potato.

Spices and Herbs

Allspice, Pimento, Jamaican Pepper A small brown berry, most commonly found here in powdered form. To really appreciate its true flavour grind the berries yourself in a coffee blender, as one of the essentials of Caribbean cooking is the use of fresh ingredients. There are hints of clove, pepper, cinnamon and nutmeg in this fragrant spice, hence its name. According to Elizabeth David it was much used in English cooking to give an aromatic scent to marinades, soused herring, salt beef and pickled pork.

Annatto Now available in this country. It is the darkish red seed of the *Bixa*, a tropical native American tree. Grind these seeds, sometimes called *roucou*, in a coffee blender.

Cardamom Seeds This seed comes from the plant of the ginger family. The small pods are greyish green in colour and are ground along with other spices for West Indian curries.

Chef's Curry Powder Packeted and sold throughout the West Indies. While normally I would always make my own combination of curry spices, I must admit that Chef's curry powder makes an absolutely characteristic West Indian curry. However, I have not seen it outside the West Indies.

Chillies There are so many varieties in the West Indies; there seems always to be a bush in someone's garden of one kind or another, red or green. Some can be small, red and look lethal but in fact just impart a fragrance with no heat. These I recommend but don't hesitate to ask first! After cutting and preparing them don't touch your face or rub your eyes as the juice remains on your fingers for hours and will burn.

Coriander Leaves This is a herb originally from the Mediterranean. The leaves are very like the large flat green parsley leaf. Both can be stored in plastic bags in the refrigerator for up to a week if kept well dry.

Curry Leaves Indians in Trinidad often have a tree in their back yard. The greyish green leaves are small and give off an aromatic scent of curry.

Garlic In the Caribbean garlic is always fresh. In England be careful to choose firm ones. As you press them there must be no hint of dryness. If using garlic for a curry it should be fried longer than in other types of cooking, but make sure it does not burn as this will taint the flavour. Try cutting a whole garlic across horizontally and see the lovely pattern. Drop both halves into the pot and in this way it slowly disintegrates and the flavour not overpowering.

Ginger The most beautiful and finest quality root ginger comes from Grenada.

Mace I shall never forget my pleasure at being handed my first ripe fruit from the nutmeg tree. In my hand lay a yellow fruit rather like a peach which once split open revealed the most brilliant lacquer-red filigree covering the nut. Very soon after its exposure it dries and loses its lustre. Store it in a sealed container and grind when needed – wonderful in salad dressings.

Nutmeg Having peeled off the mace covering you will find the hard shell of the nutmeg. In the West Indies you can cut it in half and rub a knife across its surface and it will emit the most wonderfully aromatic scent; it is fresh and oily and sensational in rum cocktails. In seventeenth and eighteenth century England people carried around their own silver nutmeg box with a grater, but nothing could rival the experience of grating it fresh from the tree. The fruit of the nutmeg tree can be boiled and made into jelly or syrup.

Parsley, Persil The flat-leaved variety is available in the West Indies. If stored dry in a plastic bag in the refrigerator it will keep for at least a week. The West Indian parsley is rather stronger in flavour than the European variety.

Peppercorns The black peppercorns are picked when immature and keep their outer skin. They are very fragrant. If they are picked when fully ripe, the covering is removed producing the white berry which is more pungent.

Pickling Spice A mixture of allspice, red hot chillies, ginger, bay leaves, mustard and coriander seeds. It is only recently that I realised this is a traditional English mixture which travelled with them to the West Indies. It is now used there to pickle chopped vegetables of all sorts in a liquid of apple cider and vinegar. It is very refreshing in the heat.

Sives, Spring Onions, Scallions These are widely used in the West Indies as there are sometimes shortages of onions there and spring onions are always available.

Tamarind This very large tropical tree bears long brown pods that grow in bunches. Inside the pod are black seeds. It is the pulp around the seeds which is used to add a piquancy to curries.

Thyme The leaf looks much the same as here and is widely used in the West Indies.

Turmeric The root of the ginger family. I have not found it fresh outside the West Indies. Dried turmeric may be substituted and gives a mild aroma and a warm yellowish colour to curries.

Techniques and Preparations

Frying Meat in Sugar and Oil

This technique is uniquely Caribbean; imbuing any stew or casserole with a particularly rich and caramelised taste which is so characteristic of West Indian cuisine.

There are two traditional ways of doing this. I personally feel the first method produces a finer flavour. Choose white sugar as it will caramelise more easily. It is also vital to dry the meat thoroughly to prevent it spluttering.

Method I

In a large saucepan pour coconut oil, (vegetable oil will make a reasonable substitute), to a depth of approximately ⅛ inch (0.25cm). Sprinkle sugar across the whole of the bottom of the pan and heat fast until the sugar turns a rich golden brown and bubbles. Be careful not to let it burn. Add the well diced meat very gently as the sugar will tend to splutter. Leave the meat for a few moments then check with a long wooden spoon to see if the meat has turned a rich brown. If necessary remove the pan from the fire to stop the sugar burning; if it burns, the dish will be bitter. Stir the meat to make sure that it has browned evenly and then cover the pan with a well-fitting lid. Leave for a few more moments but check that the meat is not darkening beyond a rich golden brown. The heat must be carefully regulated. When the meat is well browned season with salt and replace the lid and lower the heat.

¼ pint (150ml) oil with 1oz (25g) sugar will caramelise 1lb (450g) meat

Combine 1lb (450g) granulated sugar with 2 tablespoons of water. Heat until the mixture turns a rich dark brown, stirring constantly. Add ¾ pint (570ml) of cold water and boil, stirring until a syrup is formed. Allow to cool and bottle.

You can buy this syrup ready bottled and add this mixture to the meat after frying it in oil. However the taste is much more authentic if you do it yourself.

Frying Onions

One of the fundamental mistakes in English cooking is in the preparation and cooking of the humble onion. It is usually cut into large chunks, fried for a moment and served looking glassy and indigestible. For all West Indian dishes, onions should be finely chopped as they help to create the rich sauces characteristic of Caribbean cooking. Always cut the onion in half from top to bottom, lay it flat down and slice top to bottom again and then crossways. Never add meat or other ingredients until the onions are thoroughly cooked.

Seasoning

At a small hotel on the beach in St Vincent the owner used to make the most wonderful mixture of herbs and oil which he called 'sisining'. I could never get an exact account of what was in it but the smell of fresh coriander, lime juice and spices being blended was indescribable. The mixture will keep for months in the fridge and makes an excellent marinade for fish. It can also be added to meat or fish dishes during cooking to add an extra 'something'. It doesn't really matter as to exact quantities since your creative powers will be inspired by the wonderful smells of the blend and you will find that you adjust the balance to suit your taste.

1 whole bunch coriander, stalks and roots
  removed
1 large onion
6–8 spring onions

4 cloves garlic
2″ (5cm) piece fresh ginger, peeled
1 tablespoon black peppercorns
2 tablespoons oil
1 small green chilli
1 teaspoon salt
2 tablespoons malt or wine vinegar
juice ½ lemon or lime

Blend all the ingredients and refrigerate.

Sofrito

This is a seasoned yellow lard. It is made in advance and stored in the refrigerator.

1lb (450g) salted pork
¾lb (350g) annato seeds
1lb (450g) cured ham, ground
1lb (450g) cored and seeded green peppers
4oz (110g) seeded sweet chilli peppers
1lb (450g) chopped onions
6 cloves garlic
15 fresh coriander leaves, chopped
1 tablespoon dried oregano

Wash, drain and melt the salted pork in a covered pan, stirring occasionally. Remove the pork pieces. Wash and drain the annato seeds and add them to the melted lard and heat slowly for 5 minutes.

Strain the now coloured lard. In a food processor blend the ham, peppers, onions and garlic and add it to the lard. Stir in the coriander and the oregano and simmer this mixture for about half an hour.

When it has cooled pour the lard into sterilised, sealed jars and refrigerate. This will keep for about two weeks.

Coconut Milk

Coconut Milk from Fresh Coconuts

First ensure that you have a fresh coconut by shaking it; if it feels full of water, it will be good. Then split it open by dropping it on concrete – it should split neatly open into manageable size pieces. There is no need to keep the water. With a knife ease the white flesh away from the coconut wall, but don't worry about trying to remove the thin brown skin that adheres to one side. Break the flesh into small pieces and half fill your blender with it. Then fill to the top with water and blend. Repeat the process with any remaining coconut flesh. When all the flesh is quite mashed, strain the liquid through the clean cloth into a bowl; squeeze the cloth with the remains of the coconut as hard as possible. This should yield about 1 pint (570ml) of milk. You can make more by pouring another cupful of water over the remaining flesh and blending again.

Coconut Milk from Creamed Coconut

Use one third of a block of coconut cream and pour 1 pint (570ml) of boiling water over it, stir until it is completely dissolved and use.

Tinned coconut milk and dried coconut powder are available from specialist shops.

A First Taste

Avocado Soup

Try to buy a fruit without any dark blemishes on the skin. There should be no soft areas from where people have pressed them to see if they are ripe. They are now importing the smooth-skinned variety from Israel which is much better—or try those imported from Kenya.

2 medium-sized ripe avocados
½ pint (275ml) chicken stock
½ pint milk (275ml) or ¼ pint (150ml)
  evaporated milk diluted with ¼ pint (150ml)
  water
2 teaspoons olive oil
2 teaspoons coriander seeds, finely ground
1 small green pepper, finely chopped and
  seeded
2 spring onions, (scallions), very finely
  chopped
¼ teaspoon Tabasco sauce
1 tomato, skinned and seeded or 1 tablespoon
  tomato ketchup
salt and pepper, to taste

Peel and stone the avocados. Place all the ingredients, except for the salt and pepper, in a blender and work to a smooth consistency. Season to taste with salt and pepper. Chill and serve with garlic bread.

Pigs' Trotter Soup

Don't be put off by the ingredients, our forbears were not and were probably the fitter for it. In the early nineteenth century Mrs. Carmichael observed, 'that the Creole soups are very much liked by everyone and are never made with fresh meat, only salted'. A salted pig's tail or two would make an excellent substitute for the trotters.

Serves 4–6

2 pigs' trotters
1½ pints (200ml) water
3 onions, the purple Italian variety if possible
1 whole garlic bulb, cut through
   horizontally—do not remove skin
1 carrot, coarsely chopped
1 bayleaf
6 coriander seeds, coarsely crushed
1 beef stock cube
salt and black pepper, to taste
6oz (175g) Gruyère cheese

Wash the pigs' feet clean in cold running water. Place them in a large pot, add the water and bring it to the boil with the water. Remove the scum from the surface then add one finely chopped onion, garlic, carrot, bayleaf, coriander, stock cube and seasoning. Simmer for two hours.

Remove the bones and blend the soup in a liquidiser or processor. Return the blended liquid to the pot and add the cheese and the remaining onions, finely sliced.

To prevent serving strings of uncooked translucent onion try to buy the purple Italian variety and having first peeled it, place it root down on your chopping board and cut in half. Then slice the halves as thinly as possible from the top to the root and not across the grain.

Simmer for another twenty minutes and then serve.

Pumpkin Soup

Serves 4–6

2 tablespoons unsalted butter
2 onions, finely sliced
¾–1lb (350g–450g) pumpkin, peeled, seeded
    and chopped
1 stick celery, finely chopped
1 tablespoon lime or lemon juice
2 teaspoons fresh Spanish paprika
approximately 1¼ pints (700ml) chicken stock
salt and black pepper to taste
¼ teaspoon Tabasco or pepper sauce
7 fl oz (200ml) single cream or undiluted
    evaporated milk
coarsely ground black pepper, to serve
finely chopped chives or spring onion tops
    to garnish

Heat the butter in a large pan and add the onions, pumpkin and celery together with the lime or lemon juice and paprika. Don't add the pumpkin after the onion since once the onions have started cooking anything added at a lower temperature will stop them cooking and they will be indigestible and have a glassy appearance.

When the pumpkin and onion are soft, purée in the blender and add the stock, salt and Tabasco. Return to the pan and simmer for 15 minutes. Add the cream and simmer for a few more moments.

Serve with plenty of coarsely ground black pepper and some finely chopped chives or the green part of the spring onion (scallion).

Châtaigne Humus

This is a superb alternative to humus made from the customary chick peas. Chestnuts are the European equivalent of Châtaigne, the edible nuts of the West Indian tree of the same name, which is in fact related to the oak.

Serves 4–6

½lb (225g) châtaigne or chestnuts
salt and black pepper
½ pint (275ml) olive oil
1–2 cloves of garlic, peeled
2 tablespoons lime or lemon juice
single cream or evaporated milk

Make a small cut into the skin of the châtaigne or chestnuts, place in water and bring them to the boil. Drain and then cover with cold water and simmer for 20–30 minutes until they are soft.

Peel the nuts and place in a blender or processor and season. Add the olive oil, garlic and lime or lemon juice and blend. A little evaporated milk or single cream may be added to make the mixture quite smooth. The predominant taste should be the fruitiness of the olive oil and the chestnuts.

Ivan's Smoked Fish Pâté

My husband, Ivan, prepared his own smoked fish in Grenada. We found that the use of mahogany chips for the smoking imbued the food with the most wonderfully delicate flavour. We chose to smoke flying fish, which were in season.

In London there is always plenty of advice about smoking your own fish and it is well worth taking the trouble to do so. Salted herring may be substituted for the smoked fish and is also very good. Soak one medium herring over night to remove the salt and prepare in the way shown here.

This pâté makes a good introduction to any meal.

Serves 4

¼lb (110g) smoked fish of your choice, or
    salted herrings
1 clove garlic, crushed
2 small cooked potatoes, mashed
1 onion, finely chopped
4 tablespoons olive oil
black pepper and salt, to taste
2 tablespoons sour cream
1 tablespoon watercress or coriander or
    parsley, finely chopped

Place the fish, garlic, potatoes, onion, oil and seasoning in a blender or processor. Mix in the sour cream.

Garnish with the watercress, coriander or parsley. Watercress will always be found in any gutter during the rainy season in the West Indies which lasts roughly from June to December. However, even without it, it is an unusual starter to any meal. Serve with freshly baked bread.

Spiced Prawn

This is a very delicious paste to be served as a starter. I find that blending the shells in with the rest of the ingredients gives the dish a very special flavour and consistency—if you don't like the idea of the shells, make it without. The quantities of olive oil, coriander and lime juice depend rather on your own taste, but I will give some guide.

8oz (225g) prawns, unshelled
5–6 tablespoons olive oil
½ teaspoon dried thyme or 1 teaspoon fresh
   West Indian broad-leaved variety
several drops pepper sauce or Tabasco sauce
freshly squeezed juice of ⅓ lime
2 tablespoons fresh coriander leaves

Remove the heads of the prawns and put the body with its shell and all the remaining ingredients into the blender except one tablespoon of the coriander leaves.

Blend to a paste. Add more oil if it is too thick and a little salt if the prawns are not salty enough.

Serve chilled with the remainder of the finely chopped coriander sprinkled on top.

Trinidad Fried Prawns

To be sure of catching any inter-island flight it is always best to go for the first of the day around six in the morning. Although I have always found great difficulty in getting up for this there are, nevertheless, great compensations; it is still quite dark but the air is warm and a fresh wind comes down off the Northern range. Driving directly eastwards to the airport huge oxen and carts begin to appear through the white mists that hover delicately over the plain, rising and clearing as the sun approaches to reveal workers already out in the rice fields. Stalls have been set up along the roadside piled high with prawns and shrimps and other seafood in season. Very cheap and very good.

Serves 2

2 fl oz (50ml) olive oil
1 clove garlic, crushed
16–20 prawns
1½ tablespoons wine vinegar
black pepper

Use a large heavy-based frying pan and cover the bottom of the pan evenly with oil. Fry the garlic until it begins to colour taking care not to let it burn, use more oil if necessary. At this point add the prawns, the shells must not be removed even for serving as they contain the juice which is then released into the oil and vinegar. Gently warm through before pouring over the vinegar. Season with black pepper. Cover with a well-fitting lid and turn off the heat and leave for a few minutes before serving so that the juices amalgamate. Delicious with very good brown bread.

Brul Jol

I hasten to assure all who raise their eyebrows at the ingredients in this dish that as far back as 1657 they were all available in the West Indies when Richard Ligon wrote his *True and Exact History of the Island of Barbados*. He was so exact as to give us an illuminating account of the plantation near the sea run by Colonel Walrond. While his table was found wanting in good meats, the proximity of the estate to the coast of Barbados, 'supplied with all these sorts of fish, I shall name to wit, mullets, macquerals, parrat fish, snapper, red and grey, cavallos, terbums, crabs, lobsters and coney fish with divers sorts more for which we have no names'. He went on to write ' . . . his land, touching the sea but his house being not a quarter of a mile from it, and not interposed by any unlevel land, all rarities that are brought to the island, from any part of the world are taken up and brought to him . . . wine of all kinds, oyl, olives, capers, anchovies, caviar'. The list is endless. He goes on to urge us to imagine what an advantage Colonel Walrond's estate had over any inland plantation. I agree.

Here in England, some four hundred years later, we can enjoy the advantages of those ingredients which found their way to the West Indies to make this dish now known as *Brul Jol*. It is a wonderfully refreshing starter.

Serves 4

½lb (225g) salt fish, diced
6–8 spring onions, (scallions), finely chopped
1 tablespoon finely chopped parsley
2 Greek bottled peppers, (not the hot variety), finely diced
2–3 tablespoons juice from the bottled peppers
½ medium onion, finely chopped
juice half lemon
1 teaspoon Tabasco sauce
2–3 tablespoons olive oil
10 capers
6–8 olives, optional
½ large red pepper, coarsely chopped
2" (5cm) peeled cucumber, coarsely chopped
2 tomatoes, coarsely chopped

Soak the salted fish overnight, then taste a bit—if it is still too salty pour off the water and submerge it in boiling water. Tough flesh will soften and within thirty minutes or so it should be ready to use; if not, simmer it longer until it tastes less salty.

Mix all the ingredients together and chill. Serve with some freshly baked crusty bread.

Caribbean Oysters

In Jamaica we used to be able to pick oysters off the rocks, flick them open and eat them there and then.

Use fresh oysters if at all possible—if not then frozen will have to suffice. In London you may buy them from the Chinese grocery in Gerard Street—they are amazingly good value. Bought this way I defrost them very quickly by pouring boiling water over them; it takes only a matter of minutes. Then change the water several times, finally letting them soak for 5 minutes in pure lemon juice—the reason for this is that I find them, as they say in the West Indies, 'too fresh'. Rinse and dry them on a damp cloth.

Serves 2

8–12 oysters
1 tablespoon breadcrumbs per person
1 tablespoon parsley, finely chopped
1 tablespoon chives, finely chopped
4 tomatoes, skinned and chopped

¼ teaspoon pepper sauce
black pepper coarsely ground
salt
1oz (25g) unsalted butter
4 fl oz (110ml) sour cream
2 crushed anchovies, optional

Place the oysters in a shallow baking dish and sprinkle on the breadcrumbs, parsley, chives, tomatoes, pepper sauce and seasonings. Be very sparing with the black pepper and omit salt if you are going to use anchovies.

Melt the butter in the pan and mix in the sour cream, add the anchovies, if liked, and then pour it over the oysters. Bake in the oven at around 400°F/200°C/gas mark 6 for approximately 15 minutes.

This makes a superb dish on its own served with good chilled white wine and fresh brown bread or as a prelude to a special dinner. It is rich, however, and the following course should be lighter to balance it.

Mountain Chicken

What are we talking about? Ah! Frogs' legs of course, known locally as *crapaud*. This particular frog is very large and with a blackish skin; it is only to be found in the islands of Dominica and Montserrat. The usage of the local name *crapaud* is an interesting reminder that the French once held the islands; doubtless the name of Mountain Chicken came with the English occupation later on. Anyway, the Mountain Chicken lives on the cool dark slopes of the damp mountain forests and at night, especially after the rains, you may see the flickering of the *flambeaux* as the people go in search of them. Only the hind legs of the creature are eaten, the meat resembling tender chicken in texture and flavour.

Serves 4

1oz (25g) dried mushrooms
frogs' legs, 2 large or up to 6 small per
person
2 thin slices lemon or lime
white pepper
1 teaspoon celery, finely chopped
1 teaspoon parsley, finely chopped
3 tablespoons unsalted butter
1 tablespoon flour
3 egg yolks
3 tablespoons thick cream, Cornish if possible
2 teaspoons lemon juice or sherry

Rinse the mushrooms in warm water and then soak for at least one hour. Drain well and dice finely.

Cut off the frogs' legs close to the body, separate and wash thoroughly under running water. Begin at the top and strip the skin off like a glove.

Simmer the lime or lemon slices, pepper, celery, parsley, and shallots in enough water to cover the frogs' legs for 5–6 minutes. Add the frogs' legs.

When the legs are tender lift them out of the liquid and pat dry. Strain and reserve 1½ cups of this liquor. Melt the butter gently in a heavy pan and sauté the legs until light brown.

Remove them to a plate and add the mushrooms to the pan and sauté for a few minutes. Then stir the flour in gently until all the butter has been absorbed. Now slowly pour in the reserved liquor stirring constantly making sure there are no lumps. When the sauce is hot return the frogs' legs to the pan. Beat the egg yolks into the cream and stir into the sauce. Take the sauce off the heat and allow it to thicken. Add the lemon juice or sherry and serve at once.

Grande Anse Black Pudding

Living in London, it is possible to become saturated with the aural and visual arts, endless conversation and entertaining. Long periods of isolation on a West Indian island have taught me the pleasure of having time for reflection. The cool of an early Saturday evening would be a particular weekly landmark for me. After the sun had sunk below the horizon the world would be lit, for a minute or two only, by an almost internal glow—rose-hued or peach—illuminating colours of flowers and objects with an almost unbearably beautiful touch. Then darkness would fall at once bringing a sharp sense of release from the magic of those moments. That would be the hour we always chose to drive along the Grande Anse road following the edge of the waters of the Caribbean to find the black pudding lady. The glow of the fire in her iron coal pot marked her pitch beside the road. The fresh winds off the sea seemed to draw the subtly fragrant aroma of the spices in the sausages as we waited our turn while they frizzled in the lid of an old dustbin over the coal pot.

Intestines or skins, as many as you need
5 pints (2.8 litres) of blood, absolutely fresh
6–8 spring onions, (scallions), finely chopped
1–2 tablespoons parsley
1 teaspoon brown sugar
3oz (75g) salt
2 teaspoons black pepper, coarsely ground
1 liqueur glass of rum
1 teaspoon allspice, optional
3lbs (1.4kg) pork fat
3lbs (1.4kg) onions, finely diced
1¼ pints (700g) evaporated milk or thick
cream
4oz (110g) breadcrumbs (in the West Indies
   they use farine)

Soak the intestine in water in order to clean them.

Add all the seasonings, including the spring onions and rum, to the blood and stir well. Dice the fat into very small pieces and fry half the amount slowly in a very heavy pan until melted and then add the onion. Cook these until they are quite soft.

Meanwhile soak the breadcrumbs in the cream or evaporated milk. When the onions are cooked add them, the remainder of the diced fat, and the breadcrumbs in cream, to the blood. Stir thoroughly.

Rinse the intestines well and cut into suitable lenths, approximately 12" (30cms) with one end securely knotted.

Have a plastic funnel ready and place the open end of the skin carefully over the nozzle and hold tightly. Ladle the mixture into the skins. As the skins fill up they should be allowed to coil down into a chip basket. Leave enough room in the skin to allow the ingredients to swell during the cooking. Tie the ends.

Bring a large pan of water to the boil and lower the chip basket into it, having removed the pan from the heat first; this is most important as otherwise the skins will burst.

Return the pan to a very gentle heat and simmer for twenty minutes. Probe with a needle to see if they are cooked; if brown liquid results they are ready, if red liquid appears cook for a little longer. Transfer the basket to a pan of cold water still taking care the skins do not burst. Baste with oil.

It is at this stage you will see them being reheated over a charcoal brazier along the roadsides in Grenada. The charcoal adding an extra and delicious flavour to the slight sweetness of the seasoning. If no charcoal brazier is readily at hand you may use your garden barbecue!

Fish From Caribbean Waters

'We have had in a watch in the night a fish fly into a little scuttle of a cabin, no bigger than a hand of a man, a thing that might seem to some too strange for truth. The fish that does most often give this fish chase is the dolphin, which is so swift that he could not escape him ... he is no sooner mounted on wing but presently the gannet, a great fowl, lyeth, hovering aloft, and maketh ceasure of him like as one falcon.' So observed Robert Dudley in the account of his voyage to the West Indies on first sighting the exotic flying fish.

An account written in the early nineteenth century describes in glowing terms the excellence of a Trinidadian market; 'The fish market excels in convenience and beauty and regularity of anything of the sort I ever saw: when I say that it is even far superior to that of St. Peter's Port in the island of Guernsey ... the tide comes in every day and washes the whole site. In fact the market is held over the sea, the slabs are made of marble, the scales and weights accurately clean and the prices are under wise and strict regulation. The supply is abundant and for the West Indies not unreasonable.'

Sadly, 160 years on, the only market on the islands that can match up to the above description is Oistins in Barbados. Many is the time that we have spent our last few hours looking out on to the market whilst awaiting our flight home from the tropics to London. Oistins is situated on the leeward side of the island of Barbados, where the waters are lagoon like, mirroring the brightly coloured fleet of fishing vessels that moor for hundreds of yards out on the flat surface. You can sit across the road from the beach, perched on a wooden stool, and sip the last of the good rum while the sun goes down into the sea like a great palpable sear of flame and watch the silver strand of the shore and shrouding line of palms, fringe the ever darkening violet ocean. The kerosene lamps come on and it is time to stroll through the fish stalls; to be mesmerised by the wonderful sight of flying fish being filleted with breathtaking speed and precision. The temptation to buy and return to London with them is strong. Instead, we wander across the road to the wooden building that is the rum shop and bask regretfully in the soft light from the oil lamps. Outside, stars come out as only stars can come out in the bosom of the Caribbean.

On April 30th 1786, Huffman wrote in his traveller's journal, while on board ship after leaving the island of Antigua, ' . . . dolphin appeared in the water in all the liveliest tints of green and, when diving, displayed the various colours of the rainbow, intermixed with spots of azure. The last which our people took weighed eight pounds and was exceeding good eating, familiar to our cod but drier.' To this day, the variety of fish pulled from the waters of the Caribbean is astonishing. It is a common sight to see a single fisherman walking along the road from the coast with a dazzling catch strung up on a wire across his shoulder. The simplest way of buying fish when on the islands is to go to the fish market early in the morning and ask advice on the various fish available; ask how the people themselves would prepare them. The fish meat of the Caribbean is usually very much firmer than that found in northern waters and is often comparable in texture to pork or chicken. Cavali and dolphin are almost like game and can be prepared as such. Very often you will be given a slice of the head—use it to form the stock for any sauce that you may choose—it is extremely gelatinous and quite delicious. I would always ask the fisherman to scale the fish for you; if you do it yourself, beware, as some types have sharp spikes that can be lethal !

When buying fish in the tropics you should follow the same rules as anywhere else in the world. The colours should still be vivid and glistening and the eyes bright. Lift the gills on each side of the head—they should be a bright clear red. The body should be stiff and smell of the sea.

The recipes that I have included here are some of my favourites—recipes that I cook when on the islands and also try to recreate when in England. It is fun to experiment with different types of fish and important not to be overly particular in sticking rigidly to the instructions and ingredients in any one recipe. Use your instincts and imagination and you will be pleasantly surprised with the results.

Clams in Lime Juice

These shellfish are quite marvellous, served with a dash of lime juice and/or Tabasco sauce. You can buy these quite cheaply at Billingsgate. On the advice of Harrods' fishmongers I freeze them straight away—unwashed in their shells—in a sealed bag. If you should be in the happy position of having oysters, they can be prepared in this way too.

6 clams per person
lime or lemon juice, to taste
Tabasco sauce, to taste

If frozen defrost the clams half an hour before you want to eat.

Scrub them and place in a colander over simmering water. Cover the colander with a close fitting lid. Within 1–2 minutes they will open and will be done. It is very important to watch closely so that the moment they open you can remove them. If you leave them a moment longer they may be tough.

Remove the clams from the shell catching all juices in a bowl. Break off one side of the shell and discard. Replace each clam in the remaining side—first checking that the shell is free of grit.

Strain on to each clam enough of the retained juice to cover it. Add a dash of lime or lemon and if desired a drop of Tabasco sauce.

There is nothing quite like the evocative taste of fresh sea water and lime juice.

Salted Cod

Known as *bacalao* in the Spanish islands, salted cod from England was imported into the islands from the early days of slavery as part of the staple diet for the slaves and domestic servants. Today, the trade has shifted and is now plied mainly between Newfoundland in Canada and the West Indies. In return for sending down the salted fish the West Indies exports back their rum. A fine exchange.

This is a slightly tricky dish to perfect because of the unknown quality of the salted cod but when it is right it is unsurpassable. It may be varied a little by the addition of olives and garlic but this is straying back to Spain.

Serves 4

½lb (225g) salted cod
olive oil
1 large onion, finely chopped
4 tablespoons (approximately) tomato ketchup
2 dessertspoons Spanish paprika
1 tablespoon tomato juice, red wine or water
black pepper

Soak the salted cod overnight and then taste a small piece to test whether the pungency of the salty flavour has disappeared.

Coat the bottom of a large pan in oil and sprinkle in the onions. Drain the fish. The cod if it is good should flake naturally into its own segments which you should lay on top of the onions. Smear the tomato sauce and paprika evenly over the fish and then moisten the dish with the tomato juice, wine or water. Grind black pepper liberally over the top and cover with a close fitting lid. Simmer gently for approximately 45 minutes. Serve with lots of freshly baked bread.

Crab Backs

On dark nights in the West Indies, down by the sea's edge amongst the tall coconut palms you can see figures moving about carrying *flambeaux*—bottles with paraffin soaked rags stuffed down the neck to act as flares. Here in the margins between land and sea, in holes in the sand, live large crabs. The *flambeaux* carrying figures use great skill to extract these aggressive beach dwellers with machetes. If you are forced to use a more prosaic source then most markets in Britain sell live crabs. Choose smallish female ones that are heavy.

Boil a pot of water, enough to cover the crabs, and throw them in. Cook for 3–4 minutes, being careful not to overcook lest you lose all the flavour of the sea and the moistness of the flesh. Leave the crabs to cool.

To prepare, lay them on their back and take off the pointed flap and central part of the body, which is comprised of a thin bone and 'dead men's fingers'. The mouth part will come away by pressing down on it, this will leave you with the firm smooth flesh that adheres around the inside of the shell. Extract all the meat.

The beauty of crab is that you have so many ways of eating the delicious meat. You can either enjoy it as it is with chunks of fresh limes and dashes of pepper sauce, or with a bowl of fresh mayonnaise and sweet potato purée (see page 118).

You can also take the brownish-yellow meat from the rest of the shell and put it into a bowl. Then pick the meat from the legs and the claw and add any combination of the following that you most prefer; lemon or lime juice, finely chopped spring onions (scallions), finely chopped parsley, a pinch of grated mace, black pepper, olive oil, Tabasco, mayonnaise or even 1 tablespoon of breadcrumbs or sweet potato if you find the meat too rich on its own. Just mix all together, scrub out the crab back thoroughly and fill with the mixture.

Crawfish in Butter and Garlic, Grenada style

Anyone with a strong taste for crayfish would be both surprised and delighted arriving in the West Indies to find that the fast rivers cascading down through the mountain sides, lush with heavy dark green tropical vegetation, abound with crayfish.

This is how I would prepare them, both in England and in the West Indies.

Serves 2

4 crayfish
1 tablespoon unsalted butter per crayfish
2 cloves garlic, crushed
approximately 1 teaspoon lime or lemon juice
black pepper
1 tablespoon finely chopped parsley

Wash the crayfish in running water.

In a large pan melt the butter and add the garlic. Let the butter simmer at this stage but take care not to let it brown nor let the garlic change colour. Add the lemon or lime juice, (little less than a teaspoon if you are using lime).

Throw in the crayfish and grind black pepper coarsely over the dish, then sprinkle in the parsley. Simmer until the crayfish have turned pink—10 minutes at the most—they must not be overdone.

Sometimes at the last moment I turn the heat up high and let the butter brown slightly as this amalgamates with the lemon juice—it will stick slightly to the bottom of the pan and is delicious scraped off and eaten with bread.

West Indian Fish Curry in Coconut Cream Sauce

Serves 4

4 fl. oz (110ml) olive or coconut oil
1 tablespoon coriander seeds, ground
1 teaspoon mustard seeds
1 pinch cayenne pepper
6 fennel seeds, ground
6 white peppercorns, ground
black peppercorns, ground
1 cardamom pod, ground
1 teaspoon 'Chef's' curry powder or similar
1 x 14oz (400g) tin of tomatoes
1 large tomato
1 large onion
1 clove garlic
1oz (25g) coconut cream
beef stock cube
2 bay leaves
fish stock
½" (1cm) fresh root ginger, grated
4 fish steaks

In a frying pan gently fry in the oil all the spices for about ten minutes until the mustard seeds pop. In a liquidiser or processor blend the tinned tomatoes, tomato, onion and garlic together then add this to the spices with the whole bay leaves and cook slowly for 30 minutes.

Dissolve the coconut cream and the beef stock cubes in to the sauce and simmer for a further 30 minutes stirring occasionally. If the sauce becomes too thick add a cup of fish stock or water and simmer for an additional ten minutes.

Lay your fish steaks into the pan and cook them, turning once, for no more than 15 minutes. The stock cube should provide enough salt but check the seasoning at this stage. Serve with plain rice.

Fish Steaks in Cream and Lime Juice

The *Jamaica Planter* had now progressed two days out from the warm Caribbean waters. The hard violet line on the tropical horizon was becoming dark grey over the heaving seas. The ship was moving relentlessly into the Atlantic swell and the captain had taken the much debated decision to abandon the tropical whites and the crew appeared in that comforting navy uniform. Dinner was served that evening on damp white tablecloths while we clutched our glasses as the ship rolled deeply and we ate this exquisite dish.

This is a wonderfully adaptable recipe; try it with red snapper, swordfish, red mullet or any firm fleshed northern fish.

Serves 2

olive or coconut oil, enough for frying
1 large Spanish onion, finely chopped
1 clove garlic, crushed
1¼ pints (700ml) tomato juice
1 teaspoon black pepper, coarsely ground
1 tablespoon coriander seeds, coarsely ground
3–4 drops Tabasco sauce
2 teaspoons lemon or lime juice
1 teaspoon sugar
¼ pint (150ml) double cream
2 x 4–6oz (110–175g) steaks—any firm fleshed fish will do

Heat the oil and fry the onions and garlic until soft and golden. Heat the tomato juice to boiling point and add to the pan along with the black pepper, coriander seeds and Tabasco. Simmer for 15 minutes.

Stir in the lime or lemon and sugar and simmer for a further five minutes. Pour the cream into the centre of the pan and do not stir but cover and very gently simmer for five minutes more.

Place the fish steaks onto the sauce, the cream will be pushed to the edges of the dish and contrast beautifully with the rich red of the sauce around it. Cover again and cook very slowly for approximately 8–10 minutes until the steak is heated through. Tropical fish might take a little longer. Serve with plain or coconut rice.

Red Snapper in a Fiery Red Sauce

This is a very unusual sauce. Don't be put off by the use of bottled tomato sauce (which has been the cause of raised eyebrows amongst friends). It must be remembered that tomato purée and the like are rarely available in the Islands so one has to make do with what is available. The sauce also goes well with lobster.

Serves 2

4 fl oz (110ml) oil
1 large onion, finely chopped
1 dried red chilli or few drops of Tabasco
  sauce
1 tablespoon arrowroot or cornflour
7 fl oz (200ml) tomato juice
4oz (110g) tomato ketchup
1 red sweet pepper, finely chopped

1 clove garlic, crushed
1 teaspoon fresh root ginger, grated
1 teaspoon coarsely ground black pepper
½ teaspoon salt or to taste
2 teaspoons wine vinegar
2 teaspoons white sugar
1lb (450g) red snapper or trevali or in
  northern countries any firm white fish will
  do, monkfish is ideal

Heat the oil and fry the onions until they are soft and golden. Add the chilli or Tabasco.

Mix the arrowroot or cornflour with the tomato juice to make a smooth paste and add it with the tomato ketchup to the pan. Stir and simmer for three minutes. Add the remainder of the ingredients including the fish and simmer for five to ten minutes or until the oil separates from the sauce and the fish is cooked.

If absolutely fresh I would recommend steaming the fish. To prepare the fish remove head and slice the fish away from the backbone making fillets. More simply steam the whole fish—five minutes at the most each side and it will be quite easy to lift the fish meat off in sections. Serve the fish with the sauce blended and in a separate dish or place the fillets in a dish and pour the sauce over them. The secret is that because the fish is prepared separately and steamed very quickly with no seasoning the two distinct tastes of the sauce and the fish are not diminished by the other.

Serve with sweet potato or plain rice.

Red Snapper in Butter and Herbs

This fish is difficult to scale and often as not you will order steaks and end up with the task of having to scale them yourself. Be sure to ask your fishmonger to do it; you might also ask him if you could have the head—large as it might seem—it is the most beautiful pinkish red and makes the basis of an excellent soup or will freeze for future stock making.

Serves 2

2oz (50g) unsalted butter
1 tablespoon olive oil
1 spring onion, (scallion), chopped
1 clove garlic, finely crushed
1 tomato, finely chopped
red snapper steaks, ¾" (2cm) thick
salt and coarsely ground pepper, optional

Gently heat the butter in the pan and add a little olive oil to prevent it from browning and add the spring onion, garlic and chopped tomato. Barely simmer for three minutes then lay the steaks on the sauce, season very sparingly, (with such a fish as this you might try it without seasóning), and cover the pan with a very well-fitting lid.

Turn the steaks over after 4–5 minutes and cook for a further 5 minutes with the lid replaced.

This is a sensational dish. Serve with plain steamed rice.

Barbecued Squid

Squid or octopus are both easily available in West Indian waters. People go out in small open boats and spear them, or use a mask and pull them up by hand. Assuming that you are able to prepare a fire of hot glowing charcoals wherever you are, be it on a Caribbean beach or in your back garden in England you will need the following.

Serves 2

4 small squid
1 tablespoon tomato ketchup
4 fl oz (110ml) olive oil
1 clove garlic, crushed

1 tablespoon coriander leaves, chopped
2–4 drops pepper sauce or Tabasco sauce
½ teaspoon paprika
¼ teaspoon red wine vinegar
1 tablespoon (or to taste) lime or lemon juice

To clean the squid grasp the head and pull gently, the entire contents should come with it. Cut off the tentacles that grow just in front of the eyes. Feel around the opening rim of the body and you should find a hard clear plastic-like edge about ¼" (0.5cm) wide, pull it and the whole length 3–4" (7.5–10cm) should come out. Wash and dry the inside of the body carefully under running water. The body and the tentacles are ready for the fire. Cooking time is very short so have the sauce prepared before hand so that you may concentrate on the squid.

To make the sauce: stir the tomato ketchup into the olive oil until it is fairly well mixed but with still some separation making an attractive contrast. Add the remaining ingredients except for half the coriander and again do not over mix.

Cook the squid, depending on the heat, for a minimum of five minutes and a maximum of fifteen minutes. Sprinkle on the remaining coriander just before serving.

I would serve this with a salad of crisp endive and radicchio leaves, dressed with my West Indian oil dressing (see page 123) with the addition of a grated lime skin and a mould of puréed sweet potatoes and shallots.

Two Ways of Preparing Octopus

I

Cut off the tentacles just in front of the eyes, ease the head and stomach contents out of the bag and behind the eyes. Wash the tentacles thoroughly, especially checking the suckers, which can hold grit and sand. Turn the bag inside out to wash and then turn it back. Pull off the pink membrane that covers it. Rub it all over in olive oil and bake in a roasting tin for two hours on 350°F–375°F/180°C–190°C/gas mark 4–5. A little juice will exude and amalgamate with the oil.

To serve, cut the bag into even stripes across the body and the tentacles into 1″ (2.5cm) pieces; coat throughout in its own juices. Serve the same sauce as for the squid (page 49) or with lime slices.

I I

1 octopus, weighing about 1½–2lbs
  (700–900g)
7 fl oz (200ml) lemon or lime juice
2oz (50g) unsalted butter
olive oil to cook
1 clove garlic, crushed
1 pinch dried thyme
2–3 drops of Tabasco sauce
1 teaspoon freshly ground black pepper
salt, to taste

Prepare as above, but then chop the whole octopus into small pieces. Marinate the pieces for 3–4 hours in the lemon or lime juice. Melt the butter and the olive oil, discard the marinade and add the octopus and the rest of the ingredients and simmer in a well sealed pan for 1½–2 hours.

Octopus freezes very well, as soon as caught or bought put it unwashed, well wrapped into the freezer.

Tuna Steaks

This fish is nearly always available fresh in the islands, and now widely available in Britain. It is usually cut into steaks. The largest fish I have seen has been up to twenty two inches (50cm) in diameter. The flesh is like a very gamey meat and benefits from marinating overnight.

Here is a recipe for a marinade but you can also use the seasoning recipe on page 21.

Serves 4

For the marinade:

½ teaspoon salt
1 tablespoon freshly grated ginger
½ onion, finely chopped
3 spring onions, (scallions), finely chopped
1 clove garlic, chopped
¼ teaspoon West Indian pepper sauce or
   Tabasco sauce

4 tuna steaks, ¾″ (2cm) thick
2½oz (60g) flour
1 tablespoon curry powder (preferably Chef's)
salt and pepper
4 fl oz (110ml) coconut or vegetable oil

Mix the marinade ingredients together and smear the steaks with it. Leave overnight.

On a large plate mix the flour and curry powder together with the salt and pepper and dredge the steaks in it. Shake off the excess flour. Cover the bottom of a heavy frying pan with at least ⅛″ (0.25cm) of oil; the oil should be hot but not smoking. Place the steaks in the pan and do not move or shake about—this is most important when frying fish in the West Indian way, it seals in the flavour and juices and ensures that the outside becomes quite crisp. After three or four minutes, prod to see if the fish moves freely in the pan and then turn them over and cook for another few minutes.

An excellent addition to this dish can be made by adding flour to the remaining marinade juices, kneading it into small balls and frying the little dumplings at the same time as the tuna.

Turtle in the West Indies and in England

In the West Indies, the turtle is generous food certainly but honest and sophisticated. . . . At a dinner in England, it must be as they say and do in the city; turtle once and turtle throughout. A man has no heart or appetite for anything else after . . . it is more studied and elaborate, more science is shown in its anatomy . . . it is a rarity, so much acid punch and morbid soup is absorbed there. In the West Indies the turtle is a gentle alarum as from a silver trumpet blown; it is a proparascene of our manducatory energies, the regretted prophagomeron of Apicus.

So Henry Nelson Coleridge states on his observations on the preparations of the hapless beast in 1825.

The reader may well wonder why I dwell on the subject of the turtle, when it is something that very few of us are likely to see, let alone eat, but the fact is that I have seen the poor creature recently hauled from the depths of the sea, only to end up rather ignominiously on its back in the gutter gasping for air on the sunny side of the main street in Victoria, Grenada. I won't go in to how the turtle was killed suffice to say it was not unlike taking a can opener to a tin of beans, only the tin is alive! Uh! However, at that point it seemed a waste not to buy some, since no lessons would be learnt from not doing so. It was only then I realised I had absolutely no idea how to prepare it and there was no information to be found anywhere. As it is possible that travellers there will come across it I will include here a method of preparation.

Sea Turtles can reach up to a hundred pounds in weight. The green meat from the top shell is considered to be the finest, the meat taken from the bottom is white and not so highly prized. Should you find one that is small enough to handle, fill a large pan with enough sea water to cover the creature. Bring it to the boil and plunge it in, alternatively put the turtle in the water and bring it slowly to the boil. Simmer for 35–45 minutes then remove and allow it to cool on its back to keep the juices in. When cool pull the flat surface from the shell. Near the head you will find the liver and the intestines to chop into the sauce later, (or not as you prefer). Remove the meat from the shell and the skinned legs. Chop the meat into bite size pieces.

Melt some unsalted butter, add very finely chopped parsley and reheat the pieces of meat in this, now add 3 tablespoons Madeira and 7 fl oz (200ml) stock.

Serve in a large bowl.

Plantation Dishes

One of the fruits of the emancipation was the gradual succumbing of the estate houses to the forces of nature. Today with one or two exceptions you will find only ruins, however with a little imagination you can envisage the estate as it was in Mrs. Carmichael's day.

This would seem an appropriate point at which to say a few words about the redoubtable Mrs. Carmichael, whose observations on life in the West Indies will appear throughout the book. She travelled with her husband to the Caribbean in the early part of the nineteenth century, staying first on the island of St. Vincent and then on Trinidad. During her time in the islands she wrote down, very fairly, her observations on the life of the peoples there. On returning to England she offered her manuscript for publication. Sadly delays occurred in publication due to fears that her liberal views would add fuel to the abolitionist cause. Eventually, in 1833, her *Domestic Manners and Social Conditions of the White, Coloured and Negro Population of the West Indies* appeared in print.

On one side of the pasture were the negro houses. Two rows of wattled mud cottages, white-washed and thatched with cane tops; very similar in external appearance to the cottages all over Devonshire, only they have no such chimneys as are common in England ... There were some fine almond trees in the road between the negro houses, which afforded them shade during the heat of the day. The works for the manufacture of the sugar and rum, were at the foot of the hill, to the right of the house: the hill sloped gradually down to the river—an inconsiderable one, indeed, but quite sufficient even then for many useful purposes; it was beautifully clear, and some fine plantains and bananas grew on the banks. A pretty cottage stood by the waterside occupied by the watermen; it looked as white as snow, when contrasted with a deep green line of wood, which grew to a great height and served as a boundary between the Laurel Hill Estates and the Paradise Estates ... There was a winding path—which even fear of snakes and wild boars could not deter one from exploring, and which resembled exceedingly some of the lovely wild scenery of Hawthorn—den, near the village of Roslyn in Scotland.

The duties of the planter's wife seemed to be most arduous. Should the estate be way out in the country, and away from easy access to the town and markets, she would have had to rely entirely on what the estate produced. The stock and garden were her responsibilities. Everyday intrigues and jealousies were brought to her and every week the entire household linen had to be taken to the nearest running stream to be washed. Firstly the linen was beaten with lengths of wood then dashed up and down on a flat rock. I have seen these labours undergone religiously in the country regions to this very day and constantly wonder at the effort involved and how long the material would last.

Ceremonies such as the dinners and parties they gave were the only form of social intercourse. It was reckoned by visitors in those times that they never saw a servant, male or female, that would have passed as such in England! Mrs. Carmichael goes on to describe a typical colonial dinner party.

When I first arrived in the West Indies, there was little of what we call visiting "in an easy way;" family dinners, or a quiet cup of tea were unknown; ceremonious dinner parties were the only media of intercourse.

Dinner being announced about six, we were ushered into a room by no means large or lofty: two long tables were soon filled, and we sat down, in number between thirty and forty—the gentlemen greatly predominating; there was very little general conversation during dinner, and, so far as I could see, not much even between those who sat next each other. Everything looked brilliant, however, from the numerous lights (for it was already dusk), and the handsome shades, which are a great ornament to the candlesticks. The windows and doors all thrown open, displayed one of the most picturesque scenes imaginable; it was fine moonlight, and the beauty of a moonlight view in these latitudes, can be conceived by those only who have seen it. The dinner was like all West India dinners—a load of substantials, so apparently ponderous, that I instinctively drew my feet from under the table, in case it should be borne to the ground.

Turtle and vegetable soups, with fish, roast mutton (for in three days I had not seen or heard of beef, lamb, or veal), and turtle dressed in the shell, with boiled turkey, boiled fowls, a ham, mutton and pigeon pies, and stewed ducks, concluded the first course. Ducks and guinea birds, with a few ill-made puddings and tarts, &c. formed the second course. The heat of the climate formed an excuse for the indifferent pastry, and experience soon taught me that it was impossible to make light flaky pastry, such as we see every day in England. However, it must be admitted that West India cooks do not excel in the art of making sweet dishes, if I except a dish yclept "floating island," which they always succeed in admirably.

I had heard so much at home of the luxury of the West Indies, and how clever black servants were, that I looked for something not only good, but neat and even tasteful; but I was astonished to see the dishes put down without the least apparent reference to regularity, and I felt a constant inclination to put those even, that were placed awry. Many of the guests brought their servants with them, and there was therefore an immense concourse of them, of all descriptions: some with livery, and some without; some with shoes, but generally without; some wore white jackets, others were of coloured striped jean; some were young, some old; some were coloured, and others negro men; there was no arrangement, co-operation, or agreement among the servants, save only in one thing, and that was in stealing; for a bottle of wine was hardly opened, until some clever hand whipped it away, and without any apparent fear of detection or sense of shame, openly handed it out of the window to those in waiting to receive it. In short, the servants' mouths were stuffed full the whole time; and so occupied were they all in making the most of a good opportunity, that the ladies' plates would never have been changed, had it not been for the repeated and loud reproof of the gentlemen.

Such a length of time elapsed before the second course made its appearance, that I began to conclude that among the many novelties I had seen, another might be, that the servants retired to consume the remains of the first course before they again made their appearance with the second; however, after the lapse of a long, fatiguing, and silent interlude, the second course did appear, and glad was I that it was dismissed sooner than the first. A good deal of wine was drank during dinner, but not more than is usually consumed at dinner parties in England. The wine in general use in the West Indies is of the very best quality; and malt liquor, particularly London porter, acquires a degree of mildness and flavour far beyond that which it ever attains in Britain. Beer, porter, and cider, are all drank at West India dinners, but sparingly, and I apprehend these are by no means favourable to health in a tropical climate, at least to the generality of constitutions. The most general beverage, and by far the safest, is either brandy or rum and water, such as would be drank in England: the gentlemen in the West Indies make it extremely weak, about the proportion of one glass of spirits to three English pints of water:—this beverage is often rendered more agreeable to the palate by being milled,—that is, beat in a large jug or glass rummer with a long three-fingered stick, somewhat resembling a chocolate stick; this being done quickly, the liquor froths up, and forms at once the most cooling and safe beverage, whether before or after dinner. Punch was formerly much in fashion, but it is now fairly exploded, excepting by one or two old people, who naturally prefer what they were accustomed to in their youth; but these take as small a proportion of spirits in their lemonade, as the others do in water—but to return to my dinner party.

The arduous business of dinner being concluded, for the cheese was put down with the second course,—the cloth was removed, and the dessert made its appearance. It was January, and I felt somewhat astonished, when I looked at the table covered with pines, suppidilloes, pomme de rose, water lemons, grenadilloes, &c. that amidst all this, I should see nothing of the far-famed and really excellent West India preserves, so much prized in England. Just as I was meditating upon green limes and preserved ginger, the gentleman who sat next to me offered me some preserved raspberries, just come from England, by the last ship; the emphasis which was put on the word raspberries, at once shewed me that English preserves were quite as much esteemed in that country, as West India preserves are in England. I ventured to tell him how astonished I was to find that they relished our preserves, when theirs were so much superior—he assured me, that before long, I should alter my opinion: and I found this to be perfectly correct.

The ladies did not remain long at table, but soon retired to the drawing-room; . . . but there was a meagreness of conversation, which arises from an uninformed mind.

As soon as the gentlemen came in, coffee and cake were handed round, and an almost immediate bustle followed; for a heavy, though short shower of rain had fallen, and the ladies began to ponder upon the probable results of walking or riding through a miry, slippery road.

Bianca's Roast Chicken

I highly recommend this dish—the ingredients and flavours are so reminiscent of the Caribbean.

Serves 4

3–4lb (1.4–1.8kg) fresh chicken
1 lime or lemon
salt and pepper
4 cloves garlic, crushed
1 onion, quartered
1 banana, peeled
6 thin slices of lemon
olive oil
1 dessertspoon Spanish paprika
unsalted butter

For the sauce:

giblets
1 carrot, chopped
1 stick celery, chopped
1 onion, chopped
2 tablespoons parsley, finely chopped
2 cloves garlic, finely chopped
3 fl oz (75ml) olive oil
3oz (75g) unsalted butter
½ pint (275ml) boiling water
1 glass red wine
salt

Choose an absolutely fresh chicken and wash out thoroughly with lots of running water and then rub the inside with the cut surface of the lime or lemon. Rinse again and dry.

Rub salt and pepper in the cavity of the chicken and then stuff it with two crushed but not broken cloves of garlic, the onion and whole banana.

Gently push your hand between the skin and flesh of the chicken and ease it loose over the legs and back. In this space smear one crushed garlic clove and then place thin slices of butter, (⅛"–0.25cm thick and 1"–2.5cm square), and the lemon slices over each leg and across the back. Draw the skin carefully back in to place and coat the outside with olive oil, the remaining crushed garlic, paprika and salt and pepper.

Preheat the oven 450F/230C/gas mark 8 and roast for 10–15 minutes and then lower the temperature to around 325F/170C/gas mark 3 and roast for about an hour.

Meanwhile make the sauce in a heavy frying pan. Heat the oil and butter and sauté the onion, carrot, celery, parsley and garlic until softened.

Add the giblets and fry until brown. Pour in the water and wine and simmer for 40 minutes.

When the chicken is cooked add the pan juices and banana to the sauce and season. Remove the chicken neck and blend all the sauce ingredients together in a liquidiser or processor.

Discard the onion from the chicken cavity and serve this dish with sweet potato and a green salad.

Coconut Lamb

In 1844 the first ship arrived in Trinidad carrying a much needed new source of labour from the Indian continent. Over the next three years another 5,000 plus workers made the journey. They came, fell ill, deserted the estates or became destitute vagrants. By 1846 the planters and local authorities devised the indentured system to prevent desertion or illegal absence from the estates—five years work and a free passage home. Failure to meet the terms on the part of the worker resulted in a special monthly tax or imprisonment. Forced to live in squalid conditions, separated from the rest of the community, prone to disease, the Indians found themselves despised outcasts in Trinidadian society. Although mainly Hindus from the Gangetic plan, it was the minority of Muslims who instigated the celebrated festival of *Hose*, now one of the highlights of the Trinidad year. As the sugar industry was squeezed, the Indian workers found themselves moved off the estates, taking up jobs as small cultivators and becoming the pioneers of the paddy or wet rice fields. This independence allowed them to find a more settled and dignified role in society and were able to contribute to the rich cultural and political life of the island. The influence of Indian cuisine is apparent in much of modern day Trinidadian cooking and adds an extra dimension to the seemingly endless cross-fertilisation of cooking techniques and principles.

This is a most exotic dish and well worth the trouble of preparing, the delicacy of the spices is really released through the length of time the meat is left to marinate.

Serves 6

4 chillies, seeded
6 tablespoons of coriander leaves
4 cloves of garlic
2" (5cm) piece fresh root ginger
1 teaspoon salt
¾ pint (400ml) thick coconut milk (page 23)
1 boned leg of lamb, cubed (approximately 2lb–900g of meat)

6 tablespoons unsalted butter
½ fresh coconut, grated
1 tablespoon white poppy seeds
1 tablespoon cumin seeds
1 tablespoon black peppercorns
1 teaspoon turmeric (or 1"–2.5cm peeled West Indian saffron)
½ teaspoon grated nutmeg
2 medium onions, chopped
1lb (450g) potatoes, cubed

In a liquidiser blend the chillies, coriander, garlic, ginger and salt with 2–3 tablespoons of coconut milk to make a smooth paste. Marinate the lamb in this mixture for 6 hours, basting occasionally.

Melt 2 tablespoons of the butter in a frying pan and add the grated coconut, cumin seeds, poppy seeds, peppercorns, turmeric and nutmeg. Fry lightly for approximately 5 minutes. When cool liquidise this mixture with 4 fl oz (110ml) of the remaining coconut milk until it is smooth.

Melt the remaining butter in a large pan and fry the onions until they are soft and brown then stir in the coconut and spice mixture. Now add the lamb and the remainder of the coconut milk. Cover the pan and simmer. After 50 minutes add the cubed potatoes, check the seasoning and cook uncovered until the sauce has thickened and the potatoes are soft.

Serve with plain rice and sliced, boiled sweet potatoes which you have lightly fried in butter.

Two Day Lamb

The result at the end of these preparations is fit for a feast. The lamb should be succulent and falling off the bone. If neither châtaigne or chestnuts are available, unblanched almonds can be substituted.

Serves 4–6

4oz (110g) fresh root ginger
2 cloves garlic
1 tablespoon salt
zest 1 lime
2 teaspoons cumin seeds
1 tablespoon cardamom seeds
8 cloves

1 teaspoon turmeric
1½ teaspoons hot pepper or tabasco sauce
1 leg of lamb (2lb–900g meat)
7oz (200g) châtaigne or chestnuts, cooked (see Châtaigne Humus page 28)
4 tablespoons soft brown sugar
9 fl oz (250ml) yoghurt
½ teaspoon of saffron thread (soaked in 2 tablespoons of boiling water)

In a liquidiser purée the ginger, garlic, salt, zest of the lime, cumin, cardamom seeds, cloves, turmeric and pepper sauce. Make deep cuts in the lamb and rub this paste into the meat. Leave to marinate for an hour.

Purée the châtaigne or chestnuts with 2 tablespoons of sugar and half the yoghurt. Remove from the liquidiser or processor and add the rest of the yoghurt to the purée. Coat the lamb with this mixture and refrigerate for 48 hours.

Remove the lamb from the refrigerator and allow it to come to room temperature. Sprinkle with the rest of the sugar. Heat your oven to 350°F/180°C/gas mark 4 and roast the meat for 20 minutes then reduce the temperature to 325°F/170°C/gas mark 3 and leave it for 4 hours, basting occasionally.

Remove the lamb from the oven and place it in a covered serving dish and keep it in a warm place. Drain off the excess fat from the pan and stir in the saffron mixture. Boil rapidly for 20 minutes or until the sauce is reduced by half.

Serve the lamb with the sauce served separately in a jug or spooned over it. Delicious with *Creole Sweet Potatoes* or a plain purée of sweet potatoes.

Jerk Pork

Jerk Pork has evolved as a peculiarly West Indian delicacy. When I lived in Kingston, Jamaica, I was constantly allured by talk of Jerked Pork, the fabled sweetness of the dish, and that one did not know Jamaica until one had tried it. It was the speciality of the Parish of Portland, Port Antonio, on the North coast. However, to look northwards out of the back of our house was to see the Blue Mountain range climbing up and away from us in daunting majesty and grandeur. A drive across those mountains on treacherous roads, through fern-lined bamboo gorges and avoiding the oncoming sweep of the local trucks in the middle of the road was a journey undertaken only when in reckless mood.

In the seventeenth and early eighteenth century the slaves who escaped from the plantations established their own societies in the forbidding and remote mountainous regions in the north of the island of Jamaica and became known as the Maroons. It is thought that there were also a few surviving Arawak indians still and some ex-slaves that had belonged to the previous Spanish occupiers of the island. A guerrilla war ensued but the British failed to defeat them. In 1739 peace treaties followed, the terms of which, seem to me, an extraordinary achievement by the Maroons at that time. They were granted freedom, self-government, and established reservations upon which they might live. In return they had to recognise the sovereignty of the Crown and return any slaves who fled there. Prior to the signing of the treaties, the Maroon territory had been known for its wildness and dangers. The only trace to be found of them were the 'springes' that had been set to catch the wild hogs. Their skill for hog hunting spread and the historian Edward Long writing in the eighteenth century suggested their very name 'Maroon' came from the Spanish 'marrano' meaning young pig. However, the generally accepted derivation is from the term the Spanish used for escaped slaves, 'cimarrone' meaning peak dweller. There is an interesting account written in 1833 by J. B. Moreton travelling in Jamaica to the Maroon country and meeting with King Cudjo when things were more settled.

. . . he lives in a snug little house, thatched with wild pimento leaves, retired on a rugged rocky mountain covered with huge trees, in the parish of St Mary; where the wild romantic situation and the croaking of ravens and crows added much to the solemnity of the scene.

I was saluted by two centinels who were stationed at the door; king Cudjo hearing me, came out and asked me to alight, and take some refreshment; I thanked him, and as I was much fatigued, embraced his offer.

I asked him as many questions as I thought I could modestly, without giving offence, respecting his situation; he told me that he lived very happy, that he had about five thousand black subjects, commanded by his brother, Captain Davy; that they cleared odd spots of woodland, planted plenty of corn and other provisions, raised small stock, killed wild cattle, swine, &c. "I have brandy, rum and porter, (said he) make free, you are kindly welcome, I am always glad to entertain a stranger:" In short, I dined heartily, and was treated with much civility. I asked him, how he possibly could get liquors or other supplies to such a remote stupendous wilderness? "O sir, (replied he) his Majesty in England sends them to me yearly; we are very good friends: . . ."

He candidly told me, that when the island was taken by the Spaniards, his ancestors would not surrender themselves, but resolved to be free, or perish; and held out so long in the woods, that having killed several of the English, and tired the rest, a treaty of peace was concluded upon; since which time they have been loyal subjects. Different parties traverse the island, and go armed; they take up runaway negroes and bring them to their masters, for every one of which they were paid at a certain rate per mile.

When king Cudjo dies, his eldest son or Captain Davy succeeds him—he had a red coat, red breeches, a gold-laced hat, shoes, and no stockings; his wife had nothing on but an Oznabrig frock.

The hog meat was a great delicacy and needed salt in its preparation which was not obtainable in their region, by chance they discovered . . . 'a strong lixivium of wood ashes . . . by dipping their hog in the pickle which they made of them and after smoking them they were able to preserve their hog'.

After the treaties the Maroons were able to move freely to the markets and buy all the salt they needed and to sell their smoked 'jerked hog'. Henry Gosse, another traveller to the West Indies, wrote in 1851.

He was generally seen in the towns armed with a fowling piece and cutlass, and belts that suspended on one side a large plaited bag, known as a cuttacoo, and on the other a calabash, guarded with a netted covering, in which he carried his supply of water. On his back braced round his shoulders, and suspended by a bandage over the forehead, was generally seen the wicker cradle, that held a side of jerked hog, which he sold passing along, in measured slice to ready customers, as an especial delicacy to the breakfast table.

Gradually settlers moved closer to the Maroon territory and methods of preparation and cooking became diffuse. Matthew Lewis, friend of Byron and Gothic novelist, inherited estates in the West Indies and in his *Journal of a West Indian Proprietor* written in 1834 he describes a dinner.

We had at dinner a land tortoise and a barbecued pig, two of the best and richest dishes that I ever tasted:— the latter in particular, which was dressed in the true maroon fashion, being placed on a barbecue (a frame of wicker work, through whose interstices the steam can ascend), filled with peppers and spices of the highest flavour, and wrapt in plantain leaves, and then buried in a hole filled with hot stones, by whose vapor it is then baked, no particle of the juice being thus suffered to evaporate.

This method of cooking pork is still practised today or sometimes the prepared pig is smoked for a few days in a separate structure adjoining their houses.

At home in England around the same time Eliza Acton was collecting her experiences together to write her *Modern Cookery*. She lived at a very interesting time in England when the industrial revolution was changing the country from a rural to an urban society. Born in Sussex in 1799 she grew up in the country as the daughter of a brewer so she would certainly have had contact with the more basic aspects of country life. The slaughter of pigs for example, would not have been too remote an experience. I include her method for the preparation of suckling pig which makes an interesting comparison to the Jamaican style at around the same time.

After the pig has been scalded and prepared for the spit . . . (wipe it as dry as possible and put into the body about half a pint of fine breadcrumbs, mixed with three heaped teaspoonfuls of sage, minced very small, three ounces of good butter, a large saltspoonful of salt and two thirds as much of pepper and some cayenne . . . truss it as for a hare . . . rub it with butter . . . wrap it in muslin, (a good alternative to the banana leaf).

In the West Indies the men who prepare the suckling pig are called Jerk men. The dish gets its reputation for its sweetness from the pork meat itself. They rub a mixture of blood, pepper, pimento seeds, ginger, thyme, spring onions (scallions), chopped onions and salt outside and into the belly. They then wrap the entire body in pimento leaves for flavour and green banana leaves for protection. The pig weighing about 30lb is hung on green pimento sticks over a coal fire.

Roast Suckling Pig

This is my version.

10–12lb (4.6–5.5kg) suckling pig
2 tablespoons chopped fresh thyme (the broad-leaved West Indian variety, if possible or 1 tablespoon dried
1 teaspoon ground black pepper
1 teaspoon finely grated ginger
1 clove, ground
1 tablespoon freshly ground allspice
6 cloves garlic, crushed
2 bay leaves

1 tablespoon salt, to taste
7 fl oz (200ml) coconut oil
2 fl oz (50ml) lemon or lime juice

For the basting mixture:

4 fl oz (110ml) soya sauce
4 fl oz (110ml) honey
18 fl oz (500ml) dark rum

Wash the pig thoroughly both inside and out in running cold water. Dry thoroughly.

Blend all the ingredients together with the cup of oil. Rub the meat inside and out with the mixture. Refrigerate for 12 hours or overnight wrapped in foil.

Either barbecue the pig on a spit over a good fire or cook in the oven. Baste the pig constantly with the basting mixture. If you are to cook in the oven, wrap the pig in foil and cook at 325°F/170°C/gas mark 3 for 5 hours or 20 minutes per pound. For the last half an hour, remove the foil to brown the skin golden and crisp, turn the oven up to 425°F/220°C/gas mark 7—watch closely to avoid overcooking. Serve with a green banana salad (page 106).

Boucan Pork

Although the word Boucan does in fact mean smoked I have named this delightful recipe after a similar dish I had in the Boucan bar at the Trinidad Hilton.

Serves 8–10

5–6lbs (2.3–2.7kgs) leg of pork

For the marinade:

4oz (110g) soft brown sugar
3 tablespoons dark rum
6 cloves garlic
2" (5cm) fresh root ginger
4 cloves
salt and coarsely ground pepper, to taste

1 tablespoon coriander seeds
chicken stock

For the sauce:

2 fl oz (50ml) rum
2 teaspoons arrowroot
7 fl oz (200ml) stock
3 tablespoons lime or lemon juice

Thoroughly wash the pork and then score the skin diagonally at ½" (2.5cm) intervals. Blend all the marinade ingredients together in a liquidiser or processor with enough chicken stock to make a paste. Rub the paste into the joint and leave for at least an hour.

Preheat the oven to 350°F/180°C/gas mark 4 and roast the pork for 2½–3 hours. Then increase the oven temperature to crisp the skin and give it a good colour. Be careful not to burn it at this stage.

Transfer the joint to a warm serving dish and pour the pan juices into a small saucepan. Make the sauce by warming the rum in a small skillet. Remove from the heat and ignite, gently tip the skillet back and forth until the flames die out. Mix the arrowroot with the stock to make a smooth paste and then add it to the pan juices, cook gently until the sauce thickens.

Stir in the flamed rum and the lime juice and check the seasoning. Serve this dish with baked potatoes topped with sour cream and a tossed green salad with a few radicchio leaves added.

Beef in Allspice and Coconut

In the islands it is very unlikely that you will get good frozen beef from the supermarket so if at all possible try to find someone who knows a butcher in the country who is slaughtering that day. Should you go along, be prepared for some pretty hefty use of the machete or axe. Jointing meat does not really exist in the rural areas, though you can make it clear you want it for a stew or simply spot the piece you need and point. Also take care, since all meat is bludgeoned with the machete it will follow that there will be slivers of very sharp bone so wash it very carefully in water with some fresh limes and check for splinters.

Serves 4

3½ fl oz (90ml) coconut or vegetable oil
1lb (450g) good stewing beef, cubed
2 tablespoons white sugar
salt
3 fresh sprigs thyme

1 large onion, finely chopped
2 cloves garlic, crushed
black pepper
1 generous tablespoon allspice, freshly ground
7–14 fl oz (200–400ml) coconut milk (page 23) or ⅓ bar creamed coconut

Put the oil in a fairly deep saucepan and add the sugar (see page 20). Let it heat until it is a golden brown colour and bubbling. Add the meat making sure the pieces are dry otherwise the oil will splutter and the cooking temperature will be lowered.

Stir with a wooden spoon until the meat is a rich brown. Add the onions—they must be finely chopped so that they melt right down into the sauce.

Reduce the heat and add the salt. Cover the pan. At this stage all the ingredients sweat and you will be surprised at how much sauce has already been produced.

After simmering gently for 15 minutes, check to see that the onions have dissolved and add the thyme, garlic, black pepper, allspice and the coconut milk or creamed coconut. Simmer in the covered pan for an hour. Make sure it does not dry out—if necessary, add some more coconut milk or water if it seems too rich.

This dish is traditionally served with peas and rice.

West Indian Beef Stew with Armagnac or Rum

This is a dish in which I see more French than English influences. However, I have included it here as it is quite superb and well worth taking the trouble to prepare. The chief success of this dish lies in the marinade which is so characteristic of West Indian cooking, and the use of a pig's foot gives the sauce a wonderfully gelatinous quality.

You may think the use of brandy strange in West Indian cooking, but you cannot ignore the important part French culture played on the local cuisine. As Oldmixon observed in 1708 in *The British Empire in America* 'The planters seemed to depend on England and the northern colonies for a large proportion of their food. Local supplies of fresh meat, poultry, fresh fruit and milk were used by planters at their tables, while flour and breadstuff, smoked salted meats and fish and pickles, malt liquors and the like were imported. The wealthier planters even imported French brandy instead of rum for their punchies.'

In Grenada it was also possible to obtain the finest of French olive oil as is used in this recipe. The West Indian variety of thyme is more pungent, so use it if you can. Do not be alarmed by the seemingly large amount of garlic, the taste mellows in cooking.

Serves 4–6

For the marinade:

1 wine glass olive oil
1 carrot, finely diced
1 onion, finely diced
1 stick celery, finely chopped
2 shallots, (scallions), finely chopped
1 head garlic cut through horizontally
¼ pint (150ml) red wine
5 dessertspoons wine vinegar
1 tablespoon parsley, finely chopped
2–3 sprigs thyme (if you are in the West Indies dice 1½ tablespoons of the large thick-leaved variety)

1 bayleaf
black pepper and salt, to taste

For the stew:

1½lbs (700g) stewing beef, cubed
olive oil, for frying
1 pig's trotter
1 onion, finely diced
1 carrot, finely diced
1 stick celery, finely diced
1 head garlic, cut through horizontally
2–3 sprigs thyme
2 claret glasses of Armagnac or rum
½ bottle red wine
salt and pepper

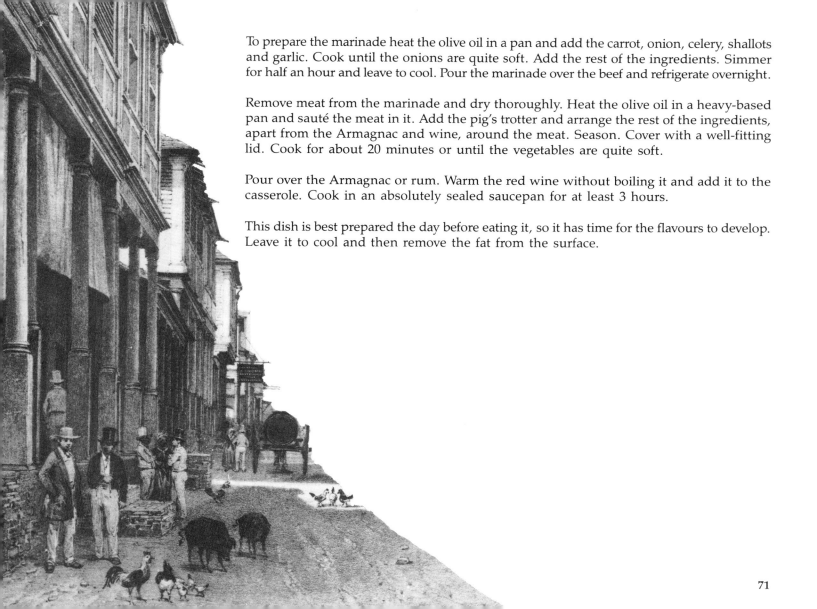

To prepare the marinade heat the olive oil in a pan and add the carrot, onion, celery, shallots and garlic. Cook until the onions are quite soft. Add the rest of the ingredients. Simmer for half an hour and leave to cool. Pour the marinade over the beef and refrigerate overnight.

Remove meat from the marinade and dry thoroughly. Heat the olive oil in a heavy-based pan and sauté the meat in it. Add the pig's trotter and arrange the rest of the ingredients, apart from the Armagnac and wine, around the meat. Season. Cover with a well-fitting lid. Cook for about 20 minutes or until the vegetables are quite soft.

Pour over the Armagnac or rum. Warm the red wine without boiling it and add it to the casserole. Cook in an absolutely sealed saucepan for at least 3 hours.

This dish is best prepared the day before eating it, so it has time for the flavours to develop. Leave it to cool and then remove the fat from the surface.

An Introduction to the Tradition of Salted Meats

The history of salted meats in the Caribbean is long and varied and is one of the best examples of the crossing over of techniques and ideas from the mother country to her newly founded colonies.

In England one of our oldest and best culinary assets was the tradition of salting meat and on its introduction to the West Indies this skill became an outstanding feature of Caribbean cooking whereas in England it is now virtually extinct. Nevertheless salted beef is still enormously popular in America especially in sandwiches, and the West Indies has never lost its taste for salting and it is still a strong influence in the preparation of local food. The salting of meat was originally largely a matter of expediency. Sir Henry Colt who sailed from Weymouth on the *Alexander* in 1632 wrote 'surely the journey is great'. He meant long of course, necessitating the preservation of foodstuffs, and it was for this reason that salted meats and fish were introduced to the islands.

J. B. Moreton in 1793 relates how a hog would have been salted.

A book keeper is obliged to superintend every domestic transaction: when a sheep or a hog is killed, he must stand by and direct a negro how to salt it: and it is very difficult to preserve meat three or four days, the best method I ever could learn, was to have a tub, (half a puncheon) with a false bottom full of holes, or a basket, supported by a few bricks, with a few gallons of water beneath; the meat should be salted well with dry salt about two or three hours after it is killed, and laid on the false bottom, or basket, and pressed well with some weight; the next day it should be rubbed well again with salt, and packed as before; the cold water beneath, though should not touch the beef, assists to extract the beef.

Today, one of the problems of using salted meat is that with the advent of refrigeration much less salt is used in the process so it is rather difficult to gauge for how long you should soak the meat. One guide could be that the larger the piece of meat the longer you soak it. Salted meats of course have less nutritional value but are enjoyed for their 'cured' flavour. The purpose of brining in a solution of salt and water preferably soft water, is to draw the natural sugars and moisture out and form lactic acids, which then protect the meat against bacteria. If the meats have been given a heavy brine or aged like old hams they must be soaked for 24 hours; you could allow 2 pints (1.1 litres) of water to 1lb (450g) of meat. Alternatively, you could place the piece of meat in a pan of cold water, bring to the boil and throw off the water and begin again.

Salted Hand of Pork

This is one of the cheapest cuts of meat available. It is not too difficult to find in market butchers; failing that, Harrods can always be relied upon to have it.

Serves 6

4–6lbs (110g–175g) salted hand of pork
2 pints (1.1 litres) medium sweet cider
6 spring onions, (scallions), finely chopped
1 stick celery, finely chopped, (in the West
   Indies be sparing with this as it is much
   stronger in flavour)
1 carrot, finely chopped
1 whole unpeeled garlic, cut through the
   sections horizontally
1 bayleaf
2–3 sprigs fresh thyme or 1 teaspoon dried
   thyme
8–10 peppercorns

Soak the pork for 6–12 hours. Ask the butcher how long it was in the brine and how old the meat was so you can judge the length of time you need to soak it.

Place the meat in a deep iron casserole with a heavy close-fitting lid and cover with cold water. Bring to the boil and skim before adding the cider and the rest of the ingredients. Now simmer for three hours.

Allow to cool in its own juices which you can later reserve to use as a stock for soup such as lentil or split pea.

Serve this succulent meat with a green banana salad garnished with a teaspoon of grated lime skin.

Should you live in the islands or are thinking of going out there, you might like to try salting your own meat. I would however recommend that you talk to your own butcher, perhaps taking note of his method particularly if you like his salted meat. The use of saltpetre must be exact, as too much can be toxic.

This method is very close to the West Indian way.

Take 1½lbs (700g) of sea salt (bay salt), 6–8oz (175g–225g) brown sugar, 1oz (25g) saltpetre and 1 gallon (4.5 litres) water and boil together for 15 minutes. Skim and strain the liquid. This will be enough to salt a 4–5lb (1.8–2.3kg) piece of beef. The meat should then be placed in to the cooled liquid, in an earthenware crock or a large covered plastic bowl. Turn daily for 9–10 days.

West Indian Souse

This time honoured dish is firmly rooted in eighteenth century England as it has as its direct antecedent a recipe from Eliza Acton called Burlington Whimsey. Souse is served in many of the islands, especially towards the end of a long evening when the atmosphere is becoming rather heady from a little too much rum. It arrives unannounced and is most welcome and surprisingly refreshing.

I daresay that the popularity of this dish is, as Mrs. Carmichael in the early eighteen hundreds says of those who have lived for some length of time in the tropics, due to the fact that 'the constitution relaxes and the desire for liquid increases. After a time one is only tempted by highly seasoned food ...' She goes on to say 'After killing a hog they keep its head and dress it ... The head and feet are cleaned and made white in strong salt water. The meat is then boiled in the salt water until quite soft. The meat is then picked off the head and placed in water well salted in lime juice sufficient to acidulate it and plenty of country peppers. It will keep for a week and is liked by everyone ... The dish is well known in the West Indies where it is called "Souse".'

1 pig's head
2 pigs' feet
½ pint (275ml) lime or lemon juice
1 tablespoon salt

For the piquant marinade:

2 hot red peppers
1 large onion, well chopped
1 green pepper, very finely chopped and
  seeded
1 red sweet pepper, very finely chopped and
  seeded
1 cucumber, peeled and thinly sliced

For the sauce:

4 tablespoons lime juice
1 cucumber, diced
¾ pint (400ml) meat stock
1 hot red pepper, chopped
salt, to taste

Have a large saucepan to take the pig's head and trotters, (ask the butcher to cut the head in half from front to back). Let them soak for a short time in fresh water—then wash well. Change the water. Add enough water to cover, add the salt and then bring to the boil.

Simmer for at least two to three hours until the meat is falling off the trotters. Remove the head and trotters onto a large board to cool. Then remove all the meat from the head, including removing the skin from the tongue and slicing. Arrange in a large bowl and cover with the stock from the cooking and add the ingredients for the piquant marinade. Cool and refrigerate for 12 hours.

Remove meats and discard marinade. Place meats into a fresh dish and cover with the sauce ingredients. Chill and serve.

A Simple and Very Quick Recipe for Salted Brisket

Wainwright and Daughter in the Fulham Rd, sell the best salted brisket that I know. It is sold in lengths about 10 inches (25cm) by 2 inches (5cm) and is not so salted that you cannot use it straightaway; remember to omit salt from the cooking.

12oz (350g) salted brisket
14 fl oz (400ml) water
2 glasses white wine
1 tablespoon parsley, very finely chopped
1 bayleaf
1 clove garlic, crushed
2–3 drops Tabasco or pepper sauce
black pepper, to taste
half a beef stock cube
¼ teaspoon sugar (optional)

Slice the beef across the grain as thinly as possible. This is easily done if it is half frozen. It must be no thicker than ⅛" (2½cm).

Simmer all the rest of the ingredients for 5 minutes. Spread the slices across the pan and simmer for approximately 30 seconds then turn and give the other side 30 seconds. Turn off the heat. I would taste it before serving sometimes it improves the dish to add a little sugar.

One Pot Meals

Today, if you make a journey in to the country in Grenada you will travel through gullys fecund with gleaming ferns and dark tropical vines, ginger lilly and hibiscus. As you climb higher and higher towards the centre of the island, valleys flow down and away like grand ravines towards the sea. Along the road, small wooden dwellings cling to the edge. The great arched leaves of the banana tree hang like loose torn rags giving shade to dusty shack yards. Here you will see people preparing their meals much as they have always done. Fires will be burning under the iron coal pot in which the whole meal will be cooked. So it was in the days when the estates were functioning. The great house would eat in much the same style as they did in England and the slaves would have to prepare their simple fare as best they could. The number of utensils would have been very limited, not to mention the ingredients. They cooked what they grew.

Mrs. Carmichael describes here the typical one-pot cooking of the slave population.

I shall now go on to describe the daily fare of the estates' negroes, beginning with the head people— that is, drivers, boiler-men, coopers, carpenters, masons, &c. These have their breakfast boiled generally the preceding evening. The mess consists of green plantains, eddoes or yam, made into soup, with an abundance of creole peas or beans, or the eddoe leaf, the calialou, or perhaps a plant which grows indigenous, and particularly among the canes; it is known by the name of weedy-weedy; I never could learn that there was any other appellation for it: it also nearly resembles spinach. This soup is seasoned with salt fish, and occasionally, as a change, with a bit of salt pork. The soup is boiled very thoroughly, and forms a substantial mess, being of the consistency of thick potatoe soup. It is well spiced with country peppers, and cooked as they cook it, is a most excellent dish indeed. All the various soups, whether tanias, calialou, pigeon pea, or pumpkin, are to be found almost daily at the tables of the white population.

The early West Indian accounts prove invaluable in picturing slave life prior to emancipation but needless to say they are very much influenced by prevailing attitudes. It is of course necessary to read between the lines, as in this account from Mrs. Carmichael.

. . . having lived in town, where I was regularly supplied with all the fruits, roots, vegetables, poultry, eggs, pork and also goat and kid, by the negro slaves, and from having walked again and again over the provision grounds of the estates. By these means I saw the whole system fully and experimentally developed. The slave may be perfectly idle, and yet he is supported. The British labourer strains every nerve to live. The slave is provided for without anxiety on his part; the object he has in view is not to live, but to save and get rich. A wife and family are often a serious burden to the British labourer, and in order to support them he is frequently obliged to seek pecuniary aid from the parish. A wife and family have been the greatest possible advantage to a slave, for his master supplied them with everything: his wife washes and cooks, the children soon begin to assist the mother, and they all work in their garden and grounds, and reap a great annual crop of different kinds.

Calaloo (callilu or calaloo)

I am fascinated with the workings and equipment of the slave kitchens. By all the accounts I've read they were simple affairs, as you would expect, yet essentially they are the same now as they were then, still producing the traditional cooking that I know and love. There were very few cooking utensils and they consisted of two or three iron pots and a strong wooden pestle and mortar which was used for beating down boiled plantain to a mash, which they called Tum Tum. They would, no doubt, have regularly cooked and eaten calaloo probably out of a calabash—the hollowed out shell of a gourd. Mrs. Carmichael in 1833 seemed to think that her husband 'enjoyed his calaloo soup as much out of a calabash as the noble man does his turtle soup in the finest chaste silver'. To this day calaloo remains one of the cornerstones of Caribbean cooking and is remembered nostalgically by all who have eaten it.

Mrs. Carmichael wrote in some detail and with affection about this great dish:

There is a well known root in Trinidad, common all over the West Indies I believe, known by the name of the eddoe. It abounds upon every estate. The roots are not unlike a rough irregular potatoe:— the leves make excellent wholesome greens; and the negro, with the addition of a bit of salt fish, or salt pork—sometimes indeed has an excellent pot of soup. He may add pigeon peas during the months they are in season; and as for capsicums—his seasoning for all dishes—they are never wanting. This soup is excellent, wholesome and palatable to all—creoles, whites, free coloured or slave; and indeed is one of the great blessings of the West Indies.

Made in a strictly traditional way or blended to a purée with good cream and parsley, this makes a delicious and unusual dish. Refer to the glossary on page 17 for the complicated explanations on the various spellings and ingredients of this recipe which has evolved over the centuries as it travelled from one island to another.

Serves 6

4–5 tablespoons vegetable oil
2 onions, finely chopped
2 cloves garlic, finely chopped

1 pinch dried thyme
¼ teaspoon freshly ground black pepper
10 okras, very finely chopped, with the
  coarse tops removed
1lb (450g) calaloo or spinach leaves,
  thoroughly washed, drained and chopped
  to ¼" (0.5cm) shreds
1 pint (570ml) coconut milk (page 23)
1 medium size cooked crab
6 spring onions, (scallions), finely chopped
¼oz (5g) salt fish, soaked overnight, skinned
  and shredded
3–4 dashes Tabasco sauce

For the puréed version:

¼ pint (150ml) good double cream (Marks
  and Spencer)
2 tablespoons well chopped parsley

Heat the oil in large saucepan and fry the chopped onions and garlic in the vegetable
oil until soft and golden. Add the thyme and the black pepper and cook for a few more
minutes. Now add the okras and the calaloo or spinach, roughly stirring to coat all the
vegetables in oil. Cook in a covered saucepan for 5 minutes. Pour in the coconut milk
and stir in the contents of the crab back with its juices and the crab legs. Add the rest
of the ingredients and simmer, well covered, for half an hour. It will all break down into
a very good rough soup. Check the seasoning.

For the sophisticated version, remove the crab legs and pick out the meat and stir it in
with half the parsley. Blend in a processor or liquidiser until absolutely smooth. Return
the soup to the stove and stir in the cream. Serve garnished with the rest of the parsley.
Superb! On a hot summer's night why not chill it before serving.

Caribbean Pilau

Around the West Indies you will sample many different versions of the same idea. This dish is said to have been originally introduced by the Moslems from India who settled mainly in Trinidad. The Spanish culture, however, is by no means lost and the rice dish Paella has strongly influenced the pilau. At any rate the pilau is certainly better in Trinidad than anywhere else in the Caribbean.

The method I have evolved is not quick but well worth the trouble. Try and keep small batches of fish stock in your freezer ready for use—the difference to one's cooking is considerable.

To make a fish stock any head of fish will do although I especially like to use salmon when it is in season. Simmer the head for twenty minutes in a pint (570ml) of water with the addition of a very finely chopped onion, half a stick of celery, one carrot, a little parsley and freshly ground pepper. Do not add salt as the whole dish is later seasoned.

Serves 4–6

1½ tablespoons duck fat or olive oil
1lb (450g) long grain rice
1 stick celery, finely chopped
2 carrots, finely chopped
2 onions, finely chopped
1 bayleaf
salt and black pepper
1 pint (570ml) fish stock
7 fl oz (200ml) soya sauce
7 fl oz (200ml) olive oil
1 tablespoon butter
12 prawns
18 oysters, if available
3 cloves garlic, crushed
¼–½lb (110–225g) firm fish, i.e. snapper, red
    fish or monkfish
4–6 chicken wings
6oz (175g) fresh peas

Heat the duck fat or olive oil and fry the rice for about 5 minutes or until the rice has absorbed the fat. Add the celery, carrots, onion, garlic, bay leaves and season sparingly. Stir gently until they are well coated in oil.

Bring the fish stock to the boil and add to the rice. The stock must be boiling otherwise the onions will seize up and become glassy. Cover the pan and cook very slowly adding more stock or water if the rice appears to have absorbed it all. When it is nearly cooked carefully stir in the soya sauce.

In half the olive oil and butter fry the seafood ingredients for approximately 3–4 minutes. Add them to the rice.

Fry the chicken pieces separately in the remainder of the oil and butter and then also add them to the rice. In the last few minutes stir in the peas—they are a surprisingly good addition.

Pepperpot

J. B. Moreton, with his genial and easy approach to travelling through the West Indies, wrote in his journal of 1790

> *When Pepper Pot and wine his blood alarms,*
> *He takes quashiba unto his arms,*
> *The melting object pleased, then takes her hoe,*
> *And works and sings till night—Tajo, Tajo*

Both married and single ladies are very dexterous at the preparing of pots, as they call them, for their husbands or lovers; a pot is a mess made of a small piece of salt pork or beef sliced, with a fowl dissected, some ocras, yams, plantains, caliloo, and plenty of fire balls, or red pepper; this inflammable, glutinous preparation is savoury, and a great provocative; they think it strengthens the back, and something else too, but in my opinion, though it stirs up the blood to force a lustful desire, it impairs the constitution; for nature when forced is impoverished; hence it is no way strange that her children are weak and sickly.

Here is a recipe from that period, the process and ingredients have not changed even today.

Dumplings, I would have thought, were a food of the past since we are all on both sides of the Atlantic a little more wary of such heavy foods. However, in the interest of authenticity, I will include the traditional method of preparing this time-honoured dish.

In the West Indies it is usual to simply mix plain flour with a little baking powder and water. The result is leaden. Don't attempt a swim for some hours after eating as you will surely sink without trace ! So that no one is taken by surprise, finding they are chewing on a red hot pepper, I would suggest that you tie the chillies to a piece of cotton.

Serves 6–8

Makes 10–12 dumplings

½lb (225g) self-raising flour
3oz (75g) shredded suet
1 teaspoon salt
¼ pint (150ml) evaporated milk or water

For the Pepperpot:

coconut or corn oil for frying
4 onions, finely chopped
2–3lbs (1–1½kg) beef or lamb, fat removed
  and cubed
½lb (225g) bacon, chopped
4 pints (2.8 litres) water
2–3 whole chilli peppers
1 green pepper, chopped
1 tablespoon paprika
salt
1 tablespoon black peppercorns, coarsely
  ground
1 small lobster
1 small crayfish
½lb (225g) cabbage, finely shredded
handful lettuce or spinach (in the West Indies
  substitute calaloo), chopped
juice 1 lemon or lime

Make the dumplings and set aside.

Heat a little coconut or corn oil and fry the onions until quite soft and golden, add the diced meat and brown gently. Once the meat is browned transfer to a large pot adding the bacon, onions, water, peppers, paprika, salt and pepper. Bring to the boil and then turn down the heat to simmer for at least 1½–2 hours.

When the meat is cooked stir in the dumplings (if you are not swimming) and then after 10 minutes add the pieces of lobster and crayfish and cabbage . After another 10 minutes sprinkle in a handful of chopped lettuce or spinach and the lime juice.

Serve almost immediately in a large soup bowl.

Pigeon Pea Soup

I remember one memorable day, I had just arrived in Grenada after a long journey from London and was taken up to a small hamlet high in the mountains for lunch. While it was being prepared I sat on the wall at the back of the house sipping my rum and reading Oscar Wilde. The sun was well up and the steam was rising up out of the folds of the valleys and the hillsides that stretched down and away from where I was sitting. A pig grunted contentedly under the house beneath me, chickens grubbed in the yard and the scent of limes and nutmegs would momentarily perfume the air around me. I reflected on the extreme pleasure of being able to enjoy and vividly feel the contrasts this earth has to offer—the sophistication and elegance of Oscar Wilde against the backcloth of sublime tropical beauty.

I was called to lunch. The great poinsettia tree with its brilliant scarlet blooms splashed against an eerily blue sky lending us shade as we ate our one pot meal.

Serves 6

½lb (225g) salt beef or pig's tail
14oz (400g) pigeon peas (if dried, soak
   overnight)
2 onions, very finely chopped
4 spring onions, (scallions), very finely
   chopped
2 cloves garlic, very finely chopped
2 sprigs thyme
salt and black pepper
coconut milk (page 23), meat stock or water to cover

Soak the salt beef for at least 2 hours to remove the salt. Drain and dice.

Wash the peas. If using dried I would spread them out first and check carefully that there are no stones, then wash them in several changes of water. Put the peas in a large iron pot, cover with water and add the diced beef and remaining ingredients. If possible I would use coconut milk or meat stock in preference to water. Cook until the peas are tender.

Rice and Peas

In Jamaica we used to be able to buy this dish ready cooked in vacuum packs from the supermarket and I have never been able to make it better. However take the time and trouble and you will get an excellent result.

Serves 6–8

1 coconut
salt
1lb (450g) rice, preferably Basmati
15oz (425g) can of red kidney beans
2–3 sprigs thyme
2 cloves garlic, crushed
black peppercorns, coarsely ground

Make the coconut milk as described on page 23. If buying rice in the islands be sure to check there are no small stones in it.

Add enough coconut milk to cover the rice. Season with salt and bring to the boil then immediately lower the heat. Cook the rice very slowly if you are using coconut milk rather than water as it will have a tendency to congeal.

As the milk is absorbed add a cup of water and the juice from the can of beans. Stir gently until that liquid is used up. Repeat this process using water until the rice is cooked. Very gently stir in the remaining ingredients.

Leave to cool and then refrigerate overnight for all the flavours to intermingle. Reheat the next day in a covered colander over a saucepan containing ½" (1cm) water.

One Pot Steamed Fish

Until recently, it was a problem to try and recreate Caribbean fish dishes authentically in the northern hemisphere. However, the markets are now selling fish flown directly from the tropics—in England from the Seychelles and in the United States from the Caribbean—and it is very good indeed, often caught only the day before.

The first time I ate fish steamed in this way was on the good ship *Olga*, travelling from St. Vincent to Trinidad. The journey should have taken ten hours or so, but we were caught in treacherously heavy seas, and finally spent two days and two nights on board. The journey was grim, especially as the ship was well loaded in excess of safety limits in order to make the trip profitable. The pathetic cargo of sheep and goats on the front decks were below water much of the way and were regularly washed overboard; we stayed in the raised stern, clinging to the side of the boat and occasionally peering down at the water thirty feet below. Our supplies of rum and food went untouched!

On the second night we all crawled under a filthy old stiffened canvas for warmth and sleep. It was one of those magical clear nights in the tropics and as I lay staring up at the stars the journey was suddenly transformed. I cannot improve on Aldous Huxley's account from *Beyond the Mexique Bay* of the same journey fifty years before:

A slowly rolling ship has a private astronomy all of its own . . . the stars would go slowly slanting up at an angle, through the sky, pause at the top of their trajectory and, with a long rush, swoop down again; then very slowly, as though tentatively, as though reluctantly, would begin to curve sideways and upwards, exploring the darkness, until at last they seemed to have found the path they were looking for, and up they would start again in a strong undeviating flight—and the whole cycle would start anew.

When dawn came, slowly and coldly, we moved back to the sides of the boat, the deck was cleared and the seamen trailed their fishing lines in the wake of the ship. The fish they hauled up were barracuda and I watched the cooking of the fish which was stewed in a very tightly covered dish—hence the name steamed—this method infused the fish with a subtle blend of spices without drowning its flavour or destroying its texture. It was one of the most delicious breakfasts I have ever eaten.

When I made this dish in my own kitchen I discovered that it was not simply our hunger, or the arduous hours of travelling which made it seem so. The fish must be absolutely fresh. Try to buy fresh red fish, cavali, king fish, jacks, trevali or red snapper. If you can only find frozen fish the texture will be more glutinous but still very good indeed.

Serves 4

4 firm-fleshed fish steaks
4 fl oz (100ml) coconut or olive oil
1 large onion, diced
2 spring onions, (scallions), diced
1 clove garlic, finely chopped
½" (1cm) fresh root ginger, finely chopped
black pepper and salt
curry powder
2–3 tablespoons tomato ketchup

Coat the bottom of a heavy based pan with a layer of oil—if possible use coconut oil for a more authentic flavour. Sprinkle in the onion, spring onion, garlic and ginger. Lay the fish in the pan without overlapping. Dust with pepper, salt and curry powder and dot with the tomato ketchup.

Cover with a well-fitting lid and stew on the lowest possible heat. Once you see the juice flowing from the fish turn the steaks. The whole cooking time should take no longer than twenty minutes.

Cumin Chicken

Serves 4–6

8–12 chicken thighs
juice 2 fresh limes
1½oz (40g) flour
1 teaspoon salt
1 teaspoon cayenne pepper
4 tablespoons butter
4½ fl oz (120ml) oil
2 teaspoons cumin seeds
2 onions, finely chopped
1″ (2.5cm) fresh root ginger, grated
2 cloves garlic, crushed
9 fl oz (250ml) yoghurt
zest of half a lime
1 tablespoon sugar

Remove the chicken skin and marinate the thighs in the lime juice for approximately one hour.

Pat the thighs dry. Mix the flour, salt and cayenne together and dust the thighs in the mixture. Heat the butter and oil and fry the chicken on a medium heat until golden. Add the cumin seeds and fry for a further 4–5 minutes. Stir in the onions, ginger and garlic and cook until the onions are soft.

Spoon in the yoghurt and add the lime zest. Bring to the boil then lower the heat and simmer until the chicken is almost falling off the bone.

This dish will have a subtle flavour of cumin seed and lime and is quite delicious served with plain rice and mango chutney.

Pimento Chicken Stew

In the West Indies we always try to choose the wings of a chicken. It is always well worth taking the trouble to singe off any feathers as the meat by the bone is so sweet—the same principle applies in Britain.

Serves 4

4 fl oz (100ml) olive oil
2oz (150g) unsalted butter
1½ tablespoons white sugar
1lb (450g) chicken wings
1 large onion, finely diced
1 clove garlic, crushed
salt, to taste
1½ teaspoons Jamaican pimento (allspice),
   ground
2 bay leaves
black pepper
¼ teaspoon chilli powder
1 fl oz (25ml) coconut cream

Melt the olive oil and butter in a pan and add the sugar (see the instructions on caramelising on page 23). Watch closely and as the mixture turns to that marvellous rich brown and just before it darkens too much, add the chicken wings, turning them so that they colour all over. Stir in the onion and garlic. Cover the pan with a very well fitting lid and turn the gas down to a moderate heat. A good deal of juice should be formed at this stage.

After about five minutes add the salt. Then add the pimento, the bay leaves, lots of coarsely ground black pepper and the chilli. Simmer for 40 minutes, stirring occasionally.

To finish, add the coconut cream and allow it to melt into the juices, stirring all the while. If the sauce is too thick, dilute with a little water.

Allspice Pork

For this recipe use pork belly or hand of pork which has a good sweet flavour.

Serves 4–6

1½lbs (700g) pork, cubed
1–1½ tablespoons white sugar
½ cup coconut or vegetable oil, for frying
1 teaspoon allspice, freshly ground
salt
1 teaspoon dried thyme or a sprig of fresh
  thyme
1 onion, finely chopped
2 cloves garlic, crushed
1 tablespoon wine vinegar
2oz (50g) coconut cream
1 pint (570ml) meat stock or water

Dry the pork cubes well and fry the meat in sugar and oil using the technique described on page 20. Add the allspice, salt and thyme. Cook for 10–15 minutes with the lid firmly on to retain the juices. Add the remaining ingredients with half the stock. Stir occasionally to see that the lumps of coconut have melted and distributed evenly.

If the sauce is too thick, add the remaining meat stock or water—stock is preferable as it greatly enhances the flavour of the dish. Serve with rice.

Chinese Pork

While the planters were ruminating on the problem of keeping the sugar estates running after emancipation and before they finally turned to India to solve the problem of cheap labour, there was China. About 2,500 Chinese arrived between 1853 and 1866. China posed many difficulties for the planters not the least of which was the considerable cost of transporting the labour from so far across the world. The Chinese came under the same indentured system as the Indians but were denied a free passage home by the planters who considered the cost too harmful to their profits. To compound the problems the Chinese themselves were not overly eager to depart for foreign lands as agricultural work at home was plentiful. Eventually the Chinese government insisted that its nationals receive a paid passage home. Consequently the scheme ceased, which was just as well as the mortality rate was high. For those Chinese who remained life improved. Unlike the East Indians who nurtured their own traditions and religion, the Chinese were more receptive to Christianity and the ways of the West. They bought out their indentures, often married Creole wives, became tradesmen and artisans and turned their back on agricultural labouring.

Here is a dish from Trinidad that shows the influence of the Chinese on the West Indies. Be sure to choose pork from the near bone for sweetness.

Serves 2–4

1lb (450g) shoulder or belly of pork, cut into small pieces
flour for dusting
2 fl oz (50ml) olive oil
2 fl oz (50ml) vegetable oil

1 large clove garlic, crushed
1 tablespoon honey
2 tablespoons soya sauce
1 tablespoon tomato ketchup
¼ teaspoon black pepper, coarsely ground
½ teaspoon pepper sauce
¼ teaspoon Chinese five spice powder

Dust the pork lightly in the flour.

Heat the two oils together in a pan and add the crushed garlic and fry. As soon as the garlic turns golden add the pork and stir well for a few minutes. Add the honey, soya sauce, tomato ketchup, black pepper, pepper sauce, Chinese spices and stir fry. In a few minutes a rich brown sauce should form. Cover the pan and simmer until the pork is tender. If the sauce becomes too thick dilute with a little water. The dish should be ready in about 30 minutes. Serve with rice and peas.

Piquant Lamb

Serves 4

1 shoulder of lamb, cut into cubes, 2–3lbs
  (1kg) of meat
olive oil, enough to cover bottom of the pan
1 tablespoon white sugar
1″ (2.5cm) fresh root ginger, grated
1 large onion, finely diced
6 cloves garlic, crushed
1 tablespoon Chef's curry powder (or similar)
1 sprig thyme, West Indian variety if possible
1 tablespoon tomato ketchup
vegetable stock cube dissolved in 15 fl oz
  (400ml) water

For the marinade:

1 large onion, diced
1 clove garlic, crushed
1 dessertspoon of wine vinegar
juice ½ a lemon
¼ teaspoon salt

Marinate the meat overnight in a covered bowl in the fridge.

Next day discard the marinade and pat the meat dry. Brown the meat in the oil and sugar until golden (see the technique on caramelising on page 20).

Add the ginger, onion, garlic, curry powder, thyme, tomato ketchup and the stock and simmer gently until the meat is tender. Serve with rice.

Spiced Lamb Trinidad

Serves 4–6

7 fl oz (200ml) yogurt
¼ teaspoon cayenne pepper or 1 teaspoon
   West Indian pepper sauce
3lb (1.3kg) leg of lamb, boned and cubed
1½" (3.5cm) fresh root ginger
4 cloves garlic
1 teaspoon white poppy seeds (optional)
1 teaspoon cumin seeds
1 tablespoon cardamom seeds

1 tablespoon black peppercorns
1 teaspoon coriander seeds
4 cloves
4 tablespoons unsalted butter
4 fl oz (100ml) vegetable oil
2 onions, chopped
1 teaspoon turmeric or 1" (2.5cm) peeled
   West Indian saffron
1 teaspoon garam masala
2 tablespoons coriander leaves, chopped

Combine the yoghurt and cayenne and coat the lamb cubes with the mixture. Marinate for 6 hours or overnight.

In a liquidiser blend the ginger, garlic, poppy seeds, cumin, cardamoms, peppercorns, coriander and cloves with 4 tablespoons of water to form a thick paste. If necessary add more water to make the paste quite smooth.

Melt the butter and oil and fry the onions until they are soft and golden. Then pour in the paste and cook gently for another 10 minutes, taking care not to let it dry out. Add the lamb cubes with the marinade, turmeric or saffron and simmer for approximately one hour, covered.

Uncover the pan and pour in ¼ cup of water. Moderately increase the heat until all the water has been absorbed then repeat the process with another ¼ cup of water stirring until it too is absorbed. Add the garam masala and coriander leaves and simmer gently for a final 25 minutes. Serve with plain rice and fried plantain.

Liver and Sour Cream

This dish is very simple and quick to prepare, a blessing in a hot climate, thus granting you more time for nursing rum punches on the veranda!

Imported frozen lambs' liver is nearly always available in the islands. If you are in the island of St. Vincent there is a shop in the town of Kingstown which sells the most subtle of locally cured smoked hams and bacon. Away from the tropics always use fresh lambs' liver and if possible the dark red onions imported in the autumn from Brittany.

Serves 2

2 large onions, the red variety or Spanish onions
lambs' liver, enough for two people
2 large potatoes

olive oil
4 slices smoked bacon
salt and black pepper, to taste
¼ teaspoon Spanish paprika
7 fl oz (200ml) cream

Slice the onions and liver very finely, (of course this is much easier if the liver is frozen). Wash but do not peel the potatoes. Slice them as close to a sixteenth of an inch (2–3mm) as possible.

Cover the bottom of a shallow pan with olive oil and then arrange the onion slices in it. Layer the potatoes on top followed by the slices of liver and bacon. Season with salt, pepper and the paprika. Cover with a close fitting lid and cook very slowly for 30 minutes or until the liver is tender. You can test it by gently piercing it with a knife, the juice should be red. Usually the liver and potatoes are ready at the same time, the potatoes remaining firm.

With this slow cooking the juices from the liver and the bacon should amalgamate with the olive oil, producing a rich sauce. Pour over the sour cream and serve.

This wonderful dish needs no accompaniment.

Stewed Oxtail

What a pleasure it can be to see a good butcher serve an oxtail; the knife cuts cleanly in to each joint of the tail with none of the usual splintering of bone that occurs when they take the hatchet to it. The tail should divide into 7 or 8 pieces and should be enough for four as it is very rich.

Serves 4

olive oil, for frying
1 whole oxtail, cut into pieces by your
   butcher
4–5 sprigs thyme, where possible fresh
   West Indian variety
1 whole garlic, unpeeled and cut horizontally
1 large onion, diced very finely
salt and black pepper, to taste
2–3 drops Tabasco or pepper sauce
1½ pints (900ml) beef stock

Heat the oil and fry the oxtail pieces in the oil in a pan with the lid tightly on. This process seals in the juice and takes approximately 20 minutes. Now add all the ingredients except for the stock. Stir and cover. You will find that a great deal of liquid is produced by this method.

When the onions have almost dissolved into the liquid bring the stock to just under boiling point and then add it to the rest of the ingredients in the pan. Cook rapidly for a moment or two then cover and simmer for 2½ hours.

Caribbean Vegetables

The islands of the Caribbean are rich in produce and offer wonderful opportunities for the enthusiastic cook. J. B. Moreton, writing in 1793, was clearly impressed with what he saw all about him:

The trees are amazing high, appearing to touch the cloud-capt towers, and are always vocal with the music of variety of birds, particularly parrots, paroquets, wood-peckers, and doves of various kinds: the mournful cooing of the latter thrills most charmingly through the ears. The woods afford shelter for vast numbers of wild cattle and swine, and some deer: I have sometimes shot a fat cattle of this kind, and frequently wild hogs; the latter are excellent when barbecued maroon fashion. The country is exceedingly fertile, and produces abundance of fruit and vegetables, such as citrons, pomegranates, Seville and China oranges, sweet and sour lemons, limes, grapes, granidilloes, pine-apples, star-apples, neeseberries, cherries, plumbs, tamarinds, pears, canipes, cocoa-nuts, bananas, water and mulk melons, water lemons, gauvas, &c. &c. and various kinds of beans and pease, cabbage, lettuce, raddish &c. with Indian and Guinea corn, yams, plantains, caffavi, &c, &c.

Labourers grew vegetables on their plots of land for their own consumption, just as did the country houses have their kitchen gardens for herbs, fruit and vegetables. The great house was supplied with all that it needed from its own land and the slaves grew a great deal of what they needed around their quarters. The interchange of food plants between continents began between the old and new world after Columbus' return from the Americas and the introduction of the first corn to Europe. Later the slave ships travelling between West Africa and the West Indies carried foodstuffs familiar to the slaves, for example pigeon peas and yams.

I was surprised to find in my research that seed selection was already a fine art in the seventeenth century thus answering my question on how plants survived their long voyages. At the turn of the eighteenth century, people who intended to settle in the islands, took their own supply of seeds from England and seemingly grew them with remarkable success. Mrs. Carmichael would give her labourers seeds from the English cabbage, turnip, carrot and peas to grow for themselves on their own plots of land.

There is not a slave upon an estate who cannot raise an abundance of fruits, roots and vegetables— far more than he can use for himself—the majority have their grounds fully stocked—they barter these for bread, salt pork, beef, corned fish, mackerel, etc., they rear great quantities of fowles, duck, guinea birds and indeed many markets are almost wholly supplied by them.

Ackee

Despite the warnings from the local people that ackee can be poisonous I can never resist it—however do not be tempted to pick the fruit of the ackee tree yourself without the advice of a local person who really knows what he is doing. The evergreen tree has its origins in West Africa and has a handsome appearance with glossy leaves. The fruit is about 3 inches (8mm) long and has a brilliant red skin that contrasts most attractively against the dark green of the leaves and the unspoilt blue of the sky. The fruit when ripe bursts open its outer red case to reveal glossy black seeds nestling in what looks like a creamy coloured brain-like structure in two sections. The fruit must be washed, the black seeds discarded and the pink tissue joining the creamy substance to the black seeds must be carefully removed as this and the seeds are highly poisonous. However, the creamy flesh has the most subtle and delicate flavour; one might liken it to lightly scrambled eggs but far more interesting. Ackee is now available in tins from specialist stores so here is a very simple recipe for its preparation.

Fried Ackee in Onions

After a very long flight from London to Barbados one cold November, I awoke on my first morning in the parish of St. James to my first breakfast of the holiday. The hotel stood beside the coral beach and the grey tired feeling faded as the beauty of the purple bouganvillea came into focus: scarlet hibiscus nodded in the cooling breeze. Ah ! the mood was indescribable and was further enhanced by aromas from the kitchen close by. We were presented with steamed sea urchin and fried ackee in onions. You can substitute white pepper for the black if you do not wish to spoil the creamy appearance of the dish.

Serves 4

2 tablespoons unsalted butter	10 ackee or 1 x 14oz (400g) tin
1 medium onion, finely chopped	black pepper and salt

Melt the butter in a pan and gently fry the onions, stirring, until they are quite soft and beginning to colour. Add the ackees to the pan and fry for approximately ten minutes turning them a few times but taking care not to break them. Season. Serve with freshly made bread.

Ackee and Salt Fish

Today you will be able to buy a packet of salted cod, salted saithe or coley at any Indian shop or in most markets and Italian delicatessens import whole sides of dried cod. If possible try and avoid the larger fish as they will be old and will need a lot of soaking. If you are in a hurry and the cod is not too tough you may pour boiling water over the dried flesh and leave it for an hour or so before flaking the fish. Otherwise soak in plenty of cold water for 12–24 hours; the length of time you leave it very much depends on its saltiness. If using the boiling water method you could pour off the water after an hour and repeat the process. Before using the fish, do taste it to see how salty it is.

Serves 4 as a main course or 6–8 as a starter

1lb (450g) salted cod
24 fresh ackee or 2 × 14oz (400g) tins
2–4 tablespoons coconut or vegetable oil
2 onions, finely chopped
2 sprigs fresh thyme or ¼ teaspoon dried
  thyme
3–4 spring onions, (scallions), finely chopped
4 tomatoes, skinned and finely chopped
black pepper

Soak the pieces of cod. While they are soaking prepare the ackee by carefully removing the black shiny pods. The edible parts are creamy yellowish, wash these taking great care they do not break up as they are very delicate. Drain them.

Heat the oil in a pan and fry the onions with the thyme until the onions have turned golden, then add the spring onions, tomatoes and black pepper. Cook this for a few more minutes before adding the cod flakes and the ackee segments. Heat through very gently and then serve with fresh bread. It makes a wonderful breakfast dish.

Avocado Salad

Elizabeth David wrote in her introduction to her recent publication on *Spices, Salt and Aromatics in the English Kitchen* that we tend to think of the avocado pear as a fruit that has only recently come into our lives. She goes on to quote from Sir Francis Colchester Wemyss who in 1931 in *The Pleasures of the Table* decided that the avocado went especially well with pressed beef. I could not agree more.

Here is his version: Make an ordinary well-seasoned oil and vinegar dressing, pour a dessertspoonful or so into the middle of each half, and then with a spoon detach the flesh into small pieces till nothing is left and the flesh is all in the centre. Mix this well with the dressing, and serve as it is, in the skin.

Delicious—but I would simply serve the avocado peeled, with stone removed and sliced quite thinly, sprinkled with a little salt and a squeeze of fresh lime juice.

Green Banana Salad

There are over one hundred cultivated varieties of this seedless fruit we know so well, (the wild varieties do have seeds). The fruit originated in east Asia, and was noted by Alexander the Great on his travels to India. They were brought to the Canary Islands by the Portuguese soon after 1400 and then imported to the West Indies. They are rich in vitamin C, and low in protein and fat, while high in carbohydrates and potassium.

When buying ripe bananas or even the unripened ones be sure to choose unblemished fruit. Like the sweet potato the fruit darkens very quickly when exposed to air; to prevent discolouration try dipping the peeled fruit into fresh lime or lemon juice, and only cut with a stainless steel knife.

I use Hellmans mayonnaise for this recipe when in the Caribbean because home-made mayonnaise is too rich and heavy in the heat of the West Indies. Hellmans is easily available out there but any good quality bought mayonnaise will do.

Serves 4

5 unblemished green bananas
3 tablespoons wine or malt vinegar
4 tablespoons good quality bought
  mayonnaise
2 tablespoons olive oil

7 fl oz (200ml) yoghurt
1 tablespoon freshly squeezed lime juice
3 spring onions, (scallions), finely chopped
1 teaspoon sugar, or to taste
1 stick celery, finely chopped
chopped walnuts (optional)
Tabasco sauce (optional)

There should be no sign of ripening or yellow colouring on the bananas. Slit the skin almost through to the flesh lengthwise and remove the ends. Place them in a pan and cover with cold water. Add the vinegar. Bring to the boil and then simmer for 20–25 minutes.

Remove the bananas from the water and allow to cool before peeling off the skin.

Mix the rest of the ingredients together in a bowl then add the chopped bananas. A handful of chopped walnuts and a dash of Tabasco sauce make an interesting addition.

Plantain

When choosing a plantain, a variety of the banana, you will find that it is only ripe when the skin is really quite black. Once peeled the fruit will be quite firm and creamy yellow in colour.

Fried Plantain

Peel the fruit; once the plantain fruit is quite blackened it becomes easy to peel. Cut the fruit in half and then slice them lengthways into at least three flat slices of approximately ¼″ (0.5cm) thick. Melt 4–6oz (110–175g) of unsalted butter and possibly a little olive oil to prevent the butter burning. Fry the slices on quite a high flame until they are golden brown. Turn and brown the other side. This is an excellent accompaniment to any dish of pork and lamb.

Boiled Plantain

This dish is less sweet and heavy than the previous recipe so would make an ideal accompaniment to a rich meal.

Choose the fruit in exactly the same way as for *Fried Plantain* but do not peel it. Cut into three or four pieces, cover with cold water and bring to the boil. Simmer for twenty minutes until a knife goes in easily. Remove from the water and allow to cool. Peel and serve plain or in a little melted butter.

Beetroot Salad

This is a wonderfully surprising salad. It incorporates ingredients from both the southern and the northern hemisphere with the Jamaica pepper (allspice) and the less exotic beetroot. As with avocado salad, it is a superb accompaniment to cold salt beef.

Serves 4

2 beetroot, cooked
approximately ¼ teaspoon salt
6–7 allspice berries, freshly ground
1 teaspoon wine vinegar
1 tablespoon parsley, finely chopped
2 tablespoons olive oil
juice half a large lime

Peel and thinly slice the beetroot and season with the rest of the ingredients except for the lime juice.

Let the dish rest for half an hour before serving—turning the beetroot two or three times. Only sprinkle the lime juice on as the dish goes on to the table allowing the tang of the citrus to stimulate the diners' senses.

Breadfruit

I lived in the island of St Vincent for the winter months on the southern most tip of the island, which caught the trade winds making it the coolest and most refreshing climate of anywhere in the entire West Indies in which to live. It had the most astonishing variation of light and in the rainy season became all the more dramatic for the sheer speed of change. I have often approached the island from the sea in the rapidly gathering dusk and noted the many columns of thin smoke curling up into the clear air. This is a sight for which St Vincent is well known—people lighting their wood fires over which they cook breadfruit for the evening meal.

"I beheld the West Indies for the first time when at sun rise, on the last day of December 1820, we anchored in the lonely bay of Calliaqua in the island of St Vincent ... I may be permitted to say that the scene that rose before me, that morning was of the most captivating kind ... I saw a succession of small valleys, covered with canes and pasturage, intermingled with slight elevations in the foreground, upon which here and there dwelling houses could be distinguished, while the prospect was terminated by mountains heaped on mountains in that wild and awful confusion that told of those awful convulsions of nature to which these tropical regions have been subjected. The sea too, such as a sea as in the temperate latitudes is rarely seen, held the island like a gem in its pure bosom ..." Mrs Carmichael, writing in 1833.

Wherever one travels in the Caribbean islands one is presented with evidence of Captain Bligh, (of the infamous Bounty), and his super human effort to be responsible for almost every variety of tree and plant from ackee to breadfruit. The mind reels at the thought of the many thousands of breadfruit trees which grow so prolifically along the length and breadth of the West Indies all coming from the one sucker Bligh took there with him on one of his voyages. It was thoughtful of him to introduce such an excellent vegetable as the breadfruit. But I doubt if even he could have imagined so much would have been attributed to him in local folklore.

The greatest gift one elderly gentleman was able to give me, was the occasional present of a breadfruit. Here you will have to understand the importance of such a gift. It cost absolutely nothing as the trees are in great abundance, but it took a good deal of observing and caring to watch that particular fruit, (one out of perhaps hundreds on the tree), until it came to the exact point of ripeness, at which point it would be presented to me as if it were a gold orb. This sometimes could be rather overwhelming since the fruit can be quite large (the size of a football). It is also difficult for two people to be inventive enough to be able to get through it all.

Baked Breadfruit

Having chosen or been presented with your whole breadfruit at the perfect state of ripeness, I would recommend baking it. Place the whole unblemished fruit in a large baking pan with some water in the bottom to prevent it from burning.

Place it in a preheated oven 375°F/190°C/gas mark 5 for approximately an hour depending on its size. Test for readiness by gently pulling on the stalk which should give easily, if it doesn't leave it a while longer.

Cut in half and either serve it as you would a baked potato with salt, pepper and butter or scoop out the flesh and mash it as in creamed potato.

For a special occasion or with a game dish you could press the baked breadfruit through a sieve and serve as you would *Pommes Mousseline*. It is quite superb, especially if you also serve the game with a spiced mango chutney.

There are other ways to prepare it but I don't think the fruit is then eaten at its best. You may peel and boil it or chip it and fry it as you would an ordinary potato.

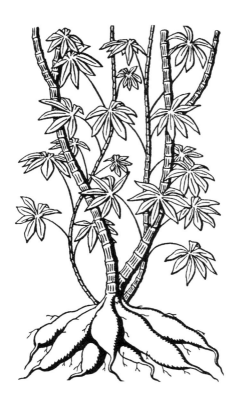

Cassava

On Raleigh's return to London he wrote that he had loved the Indians for being the greatest carousers and drunkards of the world and he encouraged his men to drink with them. The soaked cassava was chewed by the women and squirted through the teeth, the acids of the female mouth aiding the fermentation. He found it 'cleane and sweete'.

Cassava also called manioc, camioc or yucca is a tropical root vegetable; a tuberous root that is treated in a variety of different ways. It is approximately 1½" (3cm) to 10" (25cm) in length and covered with a coarse brown skin. The skin is peeled and the white flesh is washed, grated and squeezed to obtain the juice. There are two types of root: bitter (which is poisonous until cooked) and sweet. The grated meal resulting from this process is known in the north as farine and is used to thicken soups or to make puddings. Outside the tropics it is better known as tapioca. Laundry starch is also extracted from this versatile root !

Casareep

Today they make something called Casareep throughout the islands which is akin to browning. The cassava root is grated and the juice boiled down until brown and flavoured with cinnamon, cloves and brown sugar. In Guiana it is an essential ingredient in pepperpot stew. It can also be bought in bottles.

This is a simple way to make it

2lb (900g) cassava
3½ fl oz (90ml) water
¼ teaspoon ground cinnamon
¼ teaspoon ground cloves
2 teaspoons brown sugar

Peel the cassava root and chop it into pieces; wash thoroughly. Blend with the water and then squeeze through a clean cloth to extract all the liquid. The liquid should then be boiled down with the cinnamon, cloves and brown sugar. Simmer until the liquid has reduced to about a cup, stirring occasionally; it should be thick and like syrup. The extract can be stored in the refrigerator and used in other cassava recipes.

Cucumber

The cucumber is another example of the two way exchange of fruit and vegetables between the Old and New World. Columbus took it to the West Indian island of Haiti in 1494. It belongs to the squash family and there is some doubt about its origins, but it was known in China some two thousand years ago. Charlemagne cultivated cucumbers in the ninth century as did the English by the fourteenth. It was most certainly used commonly in salads in England in the seventeenth and eighteenth century. Dr. Johnson, however, did not regard it as a delicacy: 'A cucumber should be well sliced and dressed with salt and vinegar, and then thrown out as good for nothing'! Dr. Johnson clearly had not spent any time in extreme heat where a dish of freshly sliced cucumber, dressed in oil, lime juice and salt is most refreshing and stimulating to the palate.

Mrs Carmichael travelling to the West Indies seemed surprised to find the cucumber flourishing there and that the people found it agreeable.

Cucumbers grow abundantly, and are peculiarly excellent in the West Indies; they are so plentiful that they will not sell in season but out of season they will fetch a penny each. Negroes are fond of them, and taking the skin off, they eat them as we would an apple; nor are they ever found to disagree with them.

The West Indian variety is rather short and thicker in appearance than the European, but full of liquid. I was intrigued to find that Eliza Acton's recipe for cucumber below is a very close parallel to a dish prepared today in the Caribbean as a side salad.

Dressed Cucumbers

Pare and slice them very thin, strew a little salt over them, and when they have stood a little (a few minutes), drain off the water by raising one side of the dish, and letting it flow to the other; pour it away and strew more salt and a moderate seasoning of pepper on them, add two to three tablespoons of the purest salad oil, and turn the cucumbers well, the whole may receive a portion of it; then pour over it one to three dessertspoons of chilli vinegar, and a little cumin should it be needed; turn them into a clean dish and serve them.

Grenada Cucumber Salad

This is delicious as a side salad with meat or fish.

1 cucumber
2–3 tablespoons olive or vegetable oil
2–3 drops Tabasco sauce
freshly squeezed lime juice, to taste
salt and black pepper

Choose a firm, fresh cucumber with a bright green appearance. Peel and prepare the cucumber as Eliza Acton suggests above. I recommend cutting it into strips of 2″ (5cm) in length. However in place of her chilli vinegar it is customary just to toss the cucumber in oil with a squeeze or two of lime juice, Tabasco sauce and salt and pepper.

Mandrang or Mandram

It has been quite astonishing as I have continued to read recipe books and old journals of the seventeenth and eighteenth centuries to see the influences travelling back and forth between the mother country and the colonies. This is well illustrated here by Eliza Acton's *West Indian Receipt*.

Chop together very small, two moderate size cucumbers, with half the quantity of a mild onion; add the juice of a lemon a saltspoonful or more of salt a third as much of cayenne and one or two glasses of Madeira, or any other kind of dry white wine. The preparation is to be served with any kind of roast meat.

This is very close to the way we would prepare it in the West Indies. A few slices of avocado would make another welcome addition to accompany a dish of cold salt beef.

Sweet Potato

The sweet potato was known to the Incas of Peru and the Mayans of Central America long before the arrival of the Spanish conquerors. According to de Soto it was found growing in the gardens of the Indians in Louisiana in the southern states of America around 1540. It has since spread throughout the tropical world from west to east via travellers such as the Portuguese who introduced it to China, Malaya and India. In 1526 the sweet potato was introduced into Spain but it did not find the same popularity in Europe. After its arrival in England it went down in records as the 'Spanish potato' in Gerard's *Herbal*. It is a member of the Morning Glory family and we eat the tuberous root of the vine. Most of the varieties have a sweetish taste, but some match the dryness of the Irish potato.

Plain Sweet Potato

My advice is always the same when buying any fruit or vegetable—always choose those with unblemished skin and no sign of soft areas under the skin. In England today the most common variety is the West Indian potato with its darkish pink skin. Do not refrigerate but store in a cool, dark place. Eliza Acton gives excellent advice on potato preparation, 'potatoes, to boil well together, should be of the same size . . . but never scoop or apply a knife to them, even to clear the eyes . . . ' Her instructions go on to advise us to 'rinse well and arrange them compactly in a saucepan, so that they might not lie loose, and a small quantity of water will suffice to cover. Pour this in cold, and when it boils throw in one teaspoon of salt to one quart of water and then simmer the potatoes until they are nearly done, but for the last two or three minutes let them boil rapidly.'

I can recommend the same procedure for the sweet potato. Test only with a stainless steel knife, so that there is no discoloration of the flesh. Remove instantly from the water. They may be allowed to cool a little, enabling them to be handled. Peel, slice and dress in butter and serve immediately.

The cooking time may be anything from 20 minutes to 60 minutes, depending on the size of the vegetable.

Sautéed Sweet Potato

Serves 6

3lbs (1.4kg) sweet potato
6oz (175g) unsalted butter

1 clove of garlic, crushed
2–3 sprigs of thyme, West Indian variety if
    possible—otherwise use English
salt

Prepare the potatoes in exactly the same way as described above. When cooked, peel and slice into ½" (1cm) thick pieces.

Heat the butter and sauté the garlic and the thyme leaves until the garlic just starts to colour. Add the slices of potatoes and sauté for a few minutes until they have absorbed the butter. Sprinkle with a little salt just before serving.

Creole Sweet Potatoes

Serves 3–4

approximately 1lb (450g) sweet potatoes, no
    more than 2" (5cm) in diameter, peeled and
    cut into ½" (1cm) slices
juice 1 lime
2oz (50g) unsalted butter
2 tablespoons brown sugar
¼ teaspoon mace, ground
grated zest of 1 orange

Drop the sliced potatoes into cold water. Squeeze in the lime juice which will help prevent them discolouring. Boil the sweet potatoes as you would ordinary ones, taking care not to overcook them. Drain.

Arrange the potatoes in a shallow baking dish and cover with plenty of unsalted butter and the brown sugar, mace and rind of the orange. Bake in a moderate oven for approximately 30 minutes or until the sauce has formed a thick syrup.

Sweet Potato and Onion Purée

This complements most dishes.

Serves 2

1lb (450g) sweet potatoes, peeled
1 small onion or 2 small shallots, very finely
    chopped
2oz (50g) butter or enough to fry the
    onions
2 tablespoons lemon juice

Cook the sweet potatoes by placing in cold water and bringing to the boil. Simmer until a knife goes in easily.

Meanwhile fry the onions in butter until soft and golden. Drain the sweet potatoes and mash in the lemon juice and the mush of onions. Work this mixture through a sieve and serve. Alternatively, press into a greased mould and turn out to create an impressive side dish.

Pumpkin

The name seems to come from the Greek meaning melon, to which the pumpkin is a cousin. In Mexico, archaeological findings have produced fragments of the pumpkin dating back some 2,000 years, but they were probably only brought to Europe in the sixteenth century. Nowadays I think the finest variety is imported from Jamaica. It certainly has the richest yellow coloured flesh and is more fibrous than those imported from the Mediterranean.

Be sure that the flesh is firm with no dark blemishes or signs of decaying. Usually the pumpkin will already be cut into lengthways sections so that you may see the condition. Peel the dark rich green skin (I usually leave it on and eat it, except in soups) and remove the seeds.

This dish is superb with roast pork.

2lbs (900g) pumpkin, seeded and peeled
4 tablespoons brown sugar
4–6oz (110g–175g) unsalted butter

Choose a pumpkin preferably from Jamaica with a vivid gold flesh. Chop into 1″ (2.5cm) cubes. Place them in a large earthenware dish, at least 12″ (30.5cm) wide so that the cubes are evenly spread out. Sprinkle lightly with sugar and dot with lumps of butter.

Bake in a moderate oven 350F/180C/gas mark 4 for approximately 45 minutes or until soft. Serve with pork or game meat.

Dry Pumpkin Curry

Serves 4–6

2 tablespoons coconut oil
2 tablespoons unsalted butter
3 medium onions, finely chopped
3–4 drops Tabasco sauce

salt and black pepper
2 tablespoons Chef's curry powder or any
   good quality curry powder
2lb (900g) pumpkin, peeled, seeded and
   cubed

Heat the oil and butter in a large frying pan and add all the ingredients except for the
curry powder and pumpkin. Fry on a moderate heat until the onions are slightly browned.

Add the curry powder and stir for ten minutes as this will bring out the flavour. Now
mix in the pumpkin cubes and cover the pan, stirring occasionally. Cook for approximately
twenty minutes or until the pumpkin has slightly disintegrated.

Pumpkin Purée

If pumpkin is not in season swede makes an excellent substitute for this dish. It is delicious
served with roast pork and a simple green salad.

Serves 4

½lb (225g) pumpkin
4oz (110g) unsalted butter
1 medium onion, finely sliced
salt and black pepper
3½ fl oz (90ml) evaporated milk or single
   cream

Seed the pumpkin, but do not peel it, and chop finely. Melt the butter and gently fry
the pumpkin and onion in a covered pan. When the pumpkin and onion are soft, purée
them with the cream or evaporated milk in a liquidiser or processor.

Serve with plenty of coarsely ground black pepper.

Coconut and Lime Rice

There are many ways of cooking rice. The quality of rice imported into this country varies enormously, it never seems to behave the same way twice. So now I always buy Basmati which is more expensive but never disappointing or wasted. Using fresh coconut milk rather than coconut cream will produce a less cloying result.

Serves 4–6

½lb (225g) of Basmati rice
1–1½ pints (570–900ml) of coconut milk
   (page 000) or 3–4oz (75g–110g) coconut
   cream dissolved in 1¼ pints (700ml) boiling
   water
2–3 teaspoons salt
4–6 teaspoons lime juice

Wash the rice very thoroughly several times under running water. Let it soak for an hour or so in water before cooking. Drain. Just cover with the coconut milk, salt and lime juice and bring to the boil but immediately reduce to the lowest possible heat (use a special mat for this purpose). Cover with a very close-fitting lid. As the liquid is absorbed, add more milk a little at a time until the centre of the grain is soft. Cook for about 10–15 minutes.

Piquant Sauces and Pickles

Salad Oil Dressing

When you first experience the zing of the lime zest melting into the oil it will be an absolute revelation to the senses.

4½ fl oz (125ml) olive oil
scant dessertspoon lemon juice
1 teaspoon brown sugar
1 teaspoon Dijon mustard
½ teaspoon red wine vinegar
½ teaspoon freshly grated lime skin
pinch dried basil
salt and black pepper

Blend all the ingredients together and use it to coat a salad of lettuce, such as Lollo Rosso, radicchio and Batavia, skinned and chopped tomatoes, watercress, and finely chopped spring onions (scallions).

This is the only accompaniment you need to any fish steaks cooked in herbs and butter.

Green Tomato Sauce

Superb with grilled meats.

2 tablespoons vegetable oil
1 large onion, finely chopped
1lb (450g) green tomatoes, fresh or canned
2 green chillies, seeded and finely chopped
1 tablespoon coriander leaves, chopped
water or tomato juice
7 fl oz (200ml) chicken stock

Heat the oil and fry the onions until soft and well cooked. Then purée them in a blender
with the tomatoes, chillies, coriander and a little water or tomato juice. Pour this mixture
into a small pan, add the chicken stock and bring to the boil. Simmer for 15–20 minutes.
Pour into sterilised bottles.

Red Chilli Sauce

5 fresh red chillies
1 × 14oz (400g) can tomatoes
3 tablespoons water
2 fl oz (50ml) vegetable oil
1 onion, finely chopped
2 cloves garlic, crushed
1 teaspoon cumin seeds, freshly ground
4 tablespoons tomato ketchup
2 dessertspoons brown sugar
1 dessertspoon wine vinegar
1 dessertspoon Worcestershire sauce

Cut the stalk and all the seeds out of the chillies. In a processor or liquidiser purée them with the tomatoes and water.

Heat the oil in a pan and fry the onion and garlic until quite soft, then add the cumin seeds and fry for another 3–4 minutes. Add to this the blended tomato mixture and the rest of the ingredients. Simmer for ten minutes. Leave to cool. Purée the mixture again and bottle it. It will keep in the refrigerator for at least a month. It is so good in fact, that I have not been able to find out how long it might last! The first impression is of the tomatoes followed by a pleasant zing as an after taste.

Tamarind Sauce

A sauce that goes excellently with fritters or patties.

8oz (225g) tamarind
1⅓ pints (750ml) boiling water
1 teaspoon salt
1" (2.5cm) fresh root ginger, grated
2 tablespoons muscovado sugar or dark
   treacle
1 teaspoon hot chilli powder

Place the tamarind in a bowl and pour the boiling water over it. Allow to cool and using the back of a wooden spoon push through a sieve into a saucepan using as much of the soft pulp as you can, omitting the black seeds.

Stir the remaining ingredients into the pulp and simmer gently for approximately 20 minutes. It is now ready to use as an accompaniment to a meal or for refrigeration.

Banana and Date Chutney

6 bananas, peeled and chopped
4 medium onions, finely chopped
8oz (225g) dates, stoned and chopped
½ pint (275ml) malt vinegar
½ teaspoon coriander seeds, freshly ground
1" (2.5cm) fresh root ginger, freshly grated
¼ teaspoon turmeric
¼ teaspoon cumin seeds, freshly ground
½ teaspoon salt
8oz (225g) molasses or black treacle

Gently cook the bananas, onions, dates and vinegar for 15 minutes or until the onions are cooked. Then purée in a blender.

Return the purée to the pan and add the rest of the ingredients and cook on a moderate heat until the mixture is a rich brown colour—roughly 20 minutes.

Store this chutney in completely clean preserving jars in a cool dry place.

Brinjal Pickle

In Grenada there are enormous supplies of these magnificent dark purple coated vegetables so this was a very cheap pickle to make. In England however, it is rather more expensive but it is so delicious that I recommend making a small amount; its excellence will ensure that it won't last long!

3½lb (2kg) aubergines (brinjals/eggplants)
4 pints (2.3 litres) malt vinegar
1oz (25g) salt
2 pints (1.1 litres) vegetable oil
¼oz (5g) curry leaves
5oz (150g) garlic, minced
5oz (150g) fresh green ginger, (grind
   4oz–110g in a coffee blender and mince the
   remaining 1oz (25g))
2oz (50g) ground dried red chillies
1¼oz (30g) turmeric
3 dessertspoons dill seeds
3 dessertspoons cumin seeds
1lb (450g) white sugar
2oz (50g) green chillies, stalks removed,
   seeded and slit through

Wipe the aubergines clean and dry and cut them into rounds about 1" (2.5cm) thick. Place in a basin and pour over half the vinegar and the salt. Heat the oil in a thick frying pan and add the curry leaves, minced garlic and ginger, ground red chillies, turmeric, dill and cumin. Fry well until the oil rises above the mixture. Add the aubergines and the vinegar they were soaked in plus the remaining vinegar. Lastly add the sugar and the green chillies.

Stir constantly taking care not to break the vegetables. Cook for 20-30 minutes. Pour the pickle into sterilised preserving jars. This pickle is excellent with cold meat and curries.

Trinidad Pickles

4lbs (1.8kg) aubergines (eggplants/brinjals)
4 pints (2.3 litre) malt vinegar
1oz (25g) salt
2 pints (1.1 litre) oil
¼ teaspoon chilli powder
1oz (25g) turmeric
4″ (10cm) fresh root ginger, half finely
   chopped and half grated
5oz (150g) garlic, finely chopped
1½ tablespoons cumin seeds
1lb (450g) white sugar
2 green peppers, chopped

Soak the aubergine in 1 pint (570ml) of the vinegar and add the salt.

Heat the oil in the pan and add all the spices. Cook for 15–20 minutes, to an oily paste. Add the aubergines with its vinegar, sugar, the rest of the vinegar and peppers. Stir until cooked. Check for salt. Leave to cool and pour into sterilised jars.

Breads

I am going to include two basic recipes because there may be an odd occasion in the West Indies when bread is not available and these two recipes are both extraordinarily easy and successful whichever climate you may find yourself in. There is great pleasure to be had in making bread in the heat of the tropics, almost as soon as you finish kneading the dough it begins to rise and is often ready to bake in about 20 minutes.

A Good and Simple White Bread

This is very much the West Indian method of bread making which is quite different from the European way and, I think, much easier.

2lbs (900g) plain white flour
2 sachets dried yeast (Harvest Gold)
2 teaspoons salt
2 fl oz (50ml) water
2 tablespoons sugar
1 tablespoon butter
¾ pint (400ml) milk or evaporated milk

Place the flour into a large bowl and add the dried yeast and salt by just sprinkling onto the flour. Make a well. Gently heat the water, milk, sugar and butter in a pan. When the butter has melted, stir well, allow to cool and pour into the well. Knead together for 4–5 minutes. The dough should be fairly stiff.

Grease two 2lb (900g) loaf tins and divide the dough into two and press firmly down into the tins. Cover the surface with a greased plastic bag and leave to rise until double in size.

Bake in a fairly hot oven for 10–15 minutes, then lower the heat to approximately 350°F/180°C/gas mark 4 for another 50 minutes. Remove from the oven and allow to cool on a wire rack, or in cooler northern climes, return to the oven and let them cool more slowly there. This bread is superb and can be frozen very successfully.

Wholemeal Bread

To fly back home to the island of St Vincent was always a joy. The Avro Turbo-prop, forty-eight seater plane would hurtle through the turbulent warm tropical currents of air, throwing up all around us pile upon pile of white mushroom clouds that climbed heavenward as we plunged downwards towards the airstrip. From then on we held our breath as the plane veered into the winds dropping fast towards the airstrip that began at the edge of a dangerously rocky coast line. One more lurch, up and over the last of the black outcrop of rocks, and then touch down. The engines would scream as we tore to a halt. Then all would be quiet as the doors opened and in would waft the sweet damp familiar air, scented with the fumes from the coconut factory across the way. A short check through customs and we were walking away and up to the long bamboo pole that kept people, cars and animals at bay. Our small plane wheeled away from the terminal building up the runway that ran between the palm-dotted sides of the valley and, without pausing for breath, turned and raced past and away from us, up and out to sea, south towards the Grenadines. We could then, as the watch men stepped out and lifted the bamboo poles clear, walk across the runway, stop for a rum at the rum shop and then cross the road to buy and enjoy a corner-store shop that might have figured in Somerset Maugham's writings.

It was a most extraordinary shop run by a large man with a broad pale face. Being mainly of Dutch extraction he had the sort of colour that white people have who have lived their lives out in the tropics and the sun has never touched their skin; so many hours have they devoted to their businesses. In his case he provided a wonderfully unusual service in that he was quite prepared to sell the smallest possible amount of anything you might want. His fat, podgy fingers became surprisingly dexterous as he wrapped a quarter of an ounce of yeast in the smallest piece of thick unwieldy brown paper. Such a neat package and never a grain was lost from it.

3lb (1.4Kg) wholemeal flour
2 sachets dried yeast (Harvest Gold)
3 fl oz (75ml) olive or coconut oil
1 level teaspoon salt
3 teaspoons brown sugar
¾ pint (400ml) warm water

Oil two 2lb (900g) loaf tins.

Place the wholemeal brown flour in a large bowl and make a well in the centre. Add the dried yeast, oil, salt and sugar. Gradually add the water and mix to a dough. Knead for approximately 4–5 minutes.

Press the dough quite firmly into the oiled tins and leave to rise. In the chilly north it may take up to an hour and a half, in the tropics it should only take twenty minutes. When it has risen to twice its size place in a hot oven for approximately 10 to 15 minutes. Lower the temperature to 350°F/180°C/gas mark 4 for an hour.

Allow to cool for 15 minutes and the loaves should slip easily out of the tins. Let them cool slowly on a rack in the turned off oven.

Banana Bread

I have been looking for a recipe for this dark, moist banana flavoured bread ever since I tried it one glorious afternoon at the beach in Grenada. It was in mid-August when the seas are dazzling and the sun is at its highest point in the sky, the light striking the ocean causing short glass spears of emerald and sapphire to dance upon the surface of the water. Too bright to gaze upon, I sat instead with my back to the water's edge and sipped neat rum and munched banana bread. Memorable!

Of course, everybody in the islands has the 'right' recipe, but it has taken me much experimentation to exactly recreate the banana bread I enjoyed on the beach that day.

4 bananas, very ripe to the point of being
  quite brown inside the skin
2 fl oz (50ml) milk (you can also use sour or
  evaporated)
2 eggs
3oz (75g) unsalted butter, melted gently
9oz (250g) white sugar
1½ teaspoons bicarbonate of soda
½ teaspoon salt
½ teaspoon vanilla
1½ teaspoons allspice
½ teaspoon nutmeg, grated
½lb (225g) plain white flour

Blend the bananas in a food processor with the milk, eggs, melted butter and sugar. Add the remaining ingredients except for the flour.

Put the flour in a separate bowl and add the blended ingredients and mix in lightly. This amount is enough to fill a greased 2lb (900g) bread tin. Bake for approximately 1½ hours at 350F/180C/gas mark 4. Test with a knife—when ready the knife should pull out quite cleanly.

Pumpkin Bread

This is a splendid recipe; it produces a wonderfully dark moist and appetizing texture. Try and obtain the Jamaican variety of pumpkin which has a dark green skin and the richest of golden yellow centres. Alternatively, buy some tinned pumpkin or pumpkin pie mix.

1lb (450g) cooked and mashed pumpkin
10oz (275g) plain flour
2 large eggs, well beaten
4 fl oz (110ml) olive or vegetable oil
1 fl oz (25ml) water
4 oz (110g) chopped walnuts
½ teaspoon nutmeg, freshly ground
½ teaspoon cloves, freshly ground
½ teaspoon cinnamon, freshly ground
12oz (350g) brown sugar
1 teaspoon baking soda
½ teaspoon salt

If you have bought fresh pumpkin, peel and remove the seeds and fibre in the centre. Cut into small pieces and just cover with water and boil until soft. Mash as you would potatoes and then place the mixture in a large mixing bowl and add the flour and eggs. Mix in thoroughly then add the rest of the ingredients.

Bake in two, well-greased bread tins 8½ × 4½ (21 × 11cm) or four small tins. Bake at 350°F/180°C/gas mark 4 for approximately 60–70 minutes. Test the bread with a toothpick—it should be moister than ordinary bread.

Sugary Confections

It was on our arrival late one evening in Barbados that I embarked on one of the most exquisite drives of my life. We swept away from the airport in an enormous American limousine through the narrow English style country roads and across the island to a low range of hills in the north. The light had quite gone but the tropical moon was coming up, silvering the countryside with an incandescent glow. The sugar plantations fringed the edge of the road, the cane grass towering above us. That night I was eased to sleep by the local rum and what I thought was the sound of the sea below the house.

On waking the next morning, I discovered, to my astonishment, not the sea but sugar plantations stretching to the coast. The soporific sound had not been the breaking of waves but the trade winds constantly blowing through the heads of cane grass. I reflected then upon the back-breaking work of harvesting the cane; stooping and swinging a machete from dawn to dusk while suffering the flashing of the steel blades, the insects, snakes and cane lice. Nowadays the cane is often burnt first to remove both the insects and the razor sharp cane leaves—the sweet sickly smell of rum after the burning is unforgettable.

Once the cane is cut the crop is taken to the local factory to have the juice extracted, purified and condensed. When the juice has thickened by boiling in vacuum pans and kept at a temperature just below toffee-making level the molasses is thrown. The juice is transformed into a mass of pale beige crystals. This is the raw sugar. In colonial days it was more profitable to refine the sugar in Europe so that even today there are no facilities for the refining of sugar on the islands. The raw sugar is generally sold to a government agency who then sell it mainly to Tate and Lyle. Sugar trading ships bring it to England where it is refined at one of the three seaport refineries.

The crystals that so beguile us are pure sucrose, a compound which can be extracted from any vegetable matter, including grass; however the sugar cane grass is the finest source of sucrose.

Unlike spices, sugar is a comparatively recent trading product; its consumption and distribution expanded rapidly from the fifteenth to the twentieth century. The cane industry, however, was founded on human bondage. The Arawaks and the Caribs were literally worked to death by the Spaniards in their pursuit of the 'white gold'. As the power of the Spanish diminished the French, Dutch, and most notably the British, pursued this inhumanity in the form of the slave trade. The growth of the great sugar plantation estates made the fortunes of certain powerful families while the slaves who numbered nine or ten to every white man were mercilessly exploited. As the *New Statesman* reported in 1980, 'It is a substance as political as oil and has been as influential over the years in determining the world we live in'.

Although the sugar industry faltered when slavery was abolished it managed to regain its stability. Today the islands remain a sugar culture modified by coffee and bananas, or in the bigger islands, such as Jamaica and Trinidad, oil and bauxite.

Baked Bananas in their Skins

Serves 4

Choose four unblemished ripe bananas. Wipe the skin clean and put them on a metal tray in a moderate to high oven. Bake them until the skins are quite black, this usually takes about 10–15 minutes.

Serve them in their skins which you should cut through from top to bottom. You will see that the banana is of quite a different texture as this method releases the sugars in the fruit in the most temptingly aromatic way.

Serve with fresh cream or just a good rum poured over it.

Crêpes Caribe

The addition of rum and grated lime peel makes a real difference to this recipe. It is hard to be precise about the quantities, but bear in mind that the crêpe mixture should only run if you tilt it sideways in the pan. Always remember that the first crêpe seasons the pan and should be discarded.

This will make 20–30 small pancakes.

4–5oz (110–150g) butter
4–5oz (110–150g) flour
4–5oz (110–150g) sugar
2 large eggs, weighing 4–5oz (110–150g) after
   shelling
¼ pint (150ml) tepid milk
pinch salt
1 tablespoon dark rum
grated lime peel, to flavour
double cream, rum, lime juice or sugar, to
   serve

Gently melt the butter and mix it together with the flour, sugar, eggs and salt. Add the tepid milk and stir into the mixture to make a batter the consistency of double cream. There is no need in this recipe to leave the batter to stand. Just before cooking the crêpes add the rum and lime peel and stir in well. The addition of the lime and rum makes a great difference to the texture which will be much crisper, and to the flavour which will be . . . well, superb!

To cook, take a small, very heavy-based frying pan and cover the bottom lightly with butter. Heat it up and drop in one tablespoon of the batter. You will find that you have greater success if you make small pancakes. Turn them once—the sides should be golden. Serve with good double cream or perhaps rum or a little more lime juice and sugar.

Egg Yolk and Rum Dessert

Serves 4

4 egg yolks
4 tablespoons castor sugar
4 tablespoons rum
2 teaspoons grated lime rind

In a heatproof bowl beat the egg yolks and sugar together until the mixture thickens and turns pale.

Bring a saucepan a third full of water to the boil, turn down the heat and place the mixing bowl over the saucepan. Now add the rum and the grated rind to the egg and sugar mix. Beat this mixture until it rises and stiffens. Remove from the heat and serve at once in individual dishes.

The Mango

During our times in the island of Grenada, there was nothing my husband Ivan liked more than to climb the huge mango tree at the back of our house and choose the most perfect of its fruit for our breakfast. Our house, like all the others in the small eighteenth century town of St. Georges, hung against the steep hillsides that almost encircle the harbour. The back garden was below us so we were able to look out and down onto the top of the mango tree and watch it closely through its seasonal changes. Our anticipation would heighten as the cream blossoms faded and the clusters of fruit bloomed and blushed as the sun caught their cheeks.

Mrs Carmichael writing in 1833 was also clearly much struck with the fruit of the mango tree:

The fruit trees upon an estate are, by common consent, the perquisite of the negroes belonging to it. The West Indian islands differ as to their productiveness in fruit, but generally speaking, there is a great variety of fruits, according to their season; and upon every property the negroes make a considerable sum by the sale of the fruit. The mango is certainly the most abundant. This fruit hangs in such thick clusters, that the produce of one tree is immense. Of the mango there are many varieties, but the small ones are the best. Some very small delicate kinds, of a yellow colour, are to be found in the botanic garden at St Vincent; these are most delicious, though their turpentine flavour is disagreeable to those unused to it. The large kidney-shaped green mango is coarse and full of threads; and I know nothing so perfectly resembling it in taste, as a coarse field carrot, with the addition of a small portion of turpentine and sugar. Mangoes are said to produce leprosy; and I have observed that negroes who eat many of them, are very liable to cutaneous diseases.

I can safely say there is no more perfect fruit in the world; the hint of turpentine is there, indeed and only serves to make it more exotic.

The stones in the mango weigh almost more than the surrounding fruit. Four mangoes will give you about 1lb (450g) of flesh.

Mango Blancmange

The juice of any other fruit may be used instead of the mango but I would suggest trying quince. This golden, almost pear like fruit, brings a taste of the exotic to northern climes.

2 mangoes, approximately 10–12oz each
  (275g–350g)
1 pint (570ml) water
3–4oz (75–110g) sugar, or to taste
½oz (10g) gelatine, measure this carefully as a
  sachet is slightly less than ½oz (10g)
8oz (225ml) double cream

Cut the mangoes into four or five pieces leaving the skin on. Put the pieces and the seed into a large pan and add the water. Bring to the boil then simmer gently pressing with a wooden spoon until the flesh disintegrates, if the mango is slightly underripe cook just a little longer.

Have a large bowl ready and then strain the mango and liquid through a jelly bag or a muslin. If you begin the operation in the morning the juice will be there by lunchtime and the dessert will be easily ready for dinner.

When the juice is quite run through, (don't be tempted to squeeze the bag or cloth as the juice will become cloudy), put in a pan and add the sugar. Bring to the boil, lower the heat and stir in the gelatine, until thoroughly dissolved. Stir in the cream and then pour the mixture into a jelly mould which you have lightly oiled.

Allow to set in the fridge. To really appreciate the fragrance of the mango, eat the same day.

Mango Fool

Serves 4

4 mangoes
1 pint (570ml) double cream
2–3 drops Angostura bitters, optional

With a sharp knife peel and slice the mangoes. If they are very ripe there will be no need to cook them. If not steam them until soft with a very little sugar to taste, (for they are naturally sweet). At this stage you can press them through a sieve or blend them. I recommend sieving them, which although more laborious will remove the strands of fibre. When the purée is cold add the cream. Stir well and serve very cold. Two or three additional drops of Angostura bitters are an excellent improvement.

Mango Sorbet

Serves 6

3½oz (100g) granulated sugar
11 fl oz (300ml) water
14oz (400g) mango flesh
2 teaspoons lemon juice
2 egg whites

Put the sugar and the water in a heavy based pan and heat gently until the sugar dissolves. Turn up the heat and quickly bring the syrup to the boil. Remove from the heat and allow to cool completely.

Place the fruit pulp in a saucepan with 3 soupspoons of water and heat gently until completely soft. Press the pulp through a sieve and set aside.

When the sugar syrup is cold. Fold it into the mango purée with the lemon juice and pour the mixture into a bowl. Place in the freezer for 1½ hours, stirring it regularly until it sets around the edges.

Whip the egg whites until firm and fold into the contents of the bowl. Return to the freezer and allow the sorbet to set for 1 hour, then beat to eliminate the crystals. Now let the sorbet freeze undisturbed for at least 4 hours.

Cheesecake with Mango Slices

This is the most exquisite recipe and perfect for the tropics where all the ingredients are available. If cooking this dish in Britain I would suggest that you buy the cream cheese from an Italian delicatessen, where it is known as ricotta, as it is usually cheap, light and excellent. A substitute for sour cream in the tropics is to add one tablespoon of vinegar, lime or lemon juice to 7 fl oz (200ml) of evaporated milk, leaving it for 30 minutes in the fridge to go sour.

2–3 ripe 'Julie' mangoes (only available in the
    West Indies so substitute any other good
    mango or ¼lb (110g) dark red grapes)
8 digestive biscuits
1lb (450g) ricotta or curd cheese
2 eggs
white sugar, to taste
7 fl oz (200ml) sour cream
7 fl oz (200ml) yoghurt

Cut the cheeks thickly off the sides of the mangoes and slice again into ⅛" (0.25cm) slices—if using grapes, cut in half and remove the pips. Place in a bowl of water in the fridge until required.

Crush the digestive biscuits in a blender or food processor and use to line the bottom of an 8" (20cm) loose-bottomed tin.

Mix the cream cheese with the eggs and sugar until thick—be sparing with the sugar as the great pleasure of this dish lies in its refreshing sourness. Pour this mixture in blobs over the biscuit base. Spread carefully joining up the blobs to make a covering, taking care not to pull the base as you spread the mixture. Bake in the oven for 30 minutes at 350°F/180°C/gas mark 4.

Mix the sour cream, yoghurt and sugar together (again not too sweet) and pour over the base. Bake for a further 15 minutes at 250°F/130°C/gas mark ¾. When still hot arrange the mango slices or grape halves over the topping in circles. Cool in the refrigerator where the topping will set before attempting to remove from the cake tin.

Oranges in Rum with Caramel

In Aldous Huxley's little known travel book *Beyond the Mexique Bay*, written in 1934, I was fascinated to read the wariness towards buying fruit and vegetables that looked even slightly unusual was as prevalent then as it is today.

The oranges that grow in these tropical islands are particularly juicy and aromatic; but they never appear on the European market. As with so many of us, their faces are their misfortune; they have a complexion which nature has made, not orange, but bright green, irregularly marbled with yellow. Nobody, therefore, outside their country of origin will buy them. But this is not the whole story, man looks on reality through an intervening and only partially transparent medium – his language. He sees real things overlaid by their verbal symbols. Thus, when he looks at oranges, it is as though he looked at them through a stained glass window representing the orange. If the real orange corresponds with the beau ideal of oranges painted on the window he feels everything is all right. But if they don't correspond, then he becomes suspicious; something must be wrong.

This is a refreshing rather than a substantial course. If you are preparing this sweet in the West Indies I recommend you use the oranges that the Jamaicans call Ortaniques; they are thin-skinned and very juicy. They are sometimes to be found in England in the markets or at Harrods.

Serves 4–6

6 oranges, peeled	4 tablespoons soft brown sugar
4 tablespoons dark rum	2 tablespoons water

Remove as much pith as possible from the oranges and slice them into ¼" (0.5cm) slices. Remove any pips and arrange them in a bowl. Pour the rum over the slices and leave them to stand while you prepare the caramel.

Using a non stick saucepan heat the sugar and water over a high flame, stirring constantly with a wooden spoon. The more of a burnt flavour you like the longer you leave the caramel to cook. Grease a large sheet of greaseproof paper, pour the caramel onto half of it and leave to cool. Fold over the other half of the paper and hit and crush with a rolling pin until you have obtained very small chips. Spinkle the praline over the oranges. Serve chilled.

Fresh Paw Paw (Papaya)

Returning home from the West Indies on a banana boat, I awoke early to find the ship slipping almost noiselessly into the open sea between coral shores, fringed with palms, their polished spears gleaming in the early sunlight. The smells of the land had already gone and those of the ship replaced them. The seas looked quite wonderful as Jamaica retreated, the emerald waters changed to the deepest royal blue, white crested and brilliantly clear. Waves are forced up and back from the ship's prow as rainbows formed and melted in the wake of their prow. Breakfast was announced by a gong and I went below to join the Captain's table where we ate delicious chilled paw paw.

This rich fruit can be served for breakfast or as a starter to a fish dinner.

Choose a fruit with no blemishes on the skin, and which is a good consistent rich yellow all over. Skin it and remove the pips and any pith that may be in the centre. Cut into long slices, sprinkle with aromatic demerara sugar, (preferably West Indian, as it smells so strongly reminiscent of rum), and lots of fresh lime juice squeezed all over the flesh.

Chill and serve for breakfast.

The 'Princesse of Fruits' or the Pineapple

When the pineapple first reached England in Stuart times, on a particularly fast ship from the West Indies, it caused great excitement at court and became known as the 'princesse of fruits', a title coined by either Raleigh or, more probably King James who announced that, "it was a fruit too delicious for a subject to taste of". One subject who did manage to get a taste, the poet Thompson, was even inspired to ornate verse in honour of this exotic.

> *Witness, thou best Anana thou the pride*
> *of vegetable life, beyond whate'er*
> *the poets imagined in the golden age.*
> *Quick let me strip thee of thy tuft coat*
> *Spread they ambrosial stores and feast with Jove.*

This early nineteenth century dish from Hilde Leyel's *Gentle Art of Cooking* seems to capture the same spirit. Perhaps it originated in a plantation house, since it leaves the top and leaves of the fruit intact for replanting. Mrs Carmichael during her reign at the Laurel Hill Estate, Trinidad, used to please her slave labourers by cutting off the top, including the leaves so that they could plant and produce their own.

Serves 4

1 whole pineapple
1 wine glass Golden West Indian Rum

Before you start preparing the pineapple, make sure you have a large plate or bowl to hand to catch all the juices.

Cut off the bottom of the pineapple at the point where the sides begin to narrow downwards and, at the point where the sides begin to narrow upwards, cut off the top with its tuft. Then, using a very sharp knife, cut the whole of the rest of the skin away from the flesh, leaving the skin in one piece. Miss Leyel suggests that great care must be taken not to break the skin, it should come off like a hollow tube. Cut the pineapple carefully across into slices, without allowing them to fall apart, stack them together and carefully replace in the skin and stand upright in a shallow dish.

My own improvement, first made one cold December morning in London, is to add a large glass of rum to any liquor that may well have resulted from the surgery and pour it over the fruit standing in its case.

Pumpkin Pie

Very often in the Caribbean one is given a gift of a whole pumpkin. This is a superb way of preparing it. If you cannot get fresh single cream in the tropics then Nestlés tinned cream is a good substitute.

Serves 4−6

6oz (175g) shortcrust pastry
1½lbs (700g) pumpkin, puréed
1½ teaspoons cinnamon, freshly ground
¼ teaspoon cloves, ground together with the
  cinnamon
½ teaspoon fresh ginger
4oz (110g) dark demerara sugar
1½ teaspoons salt
3 eggs, lightly beaten
9 fl oz (250ml) single cream

Roll the pastry to ¼" (0.5cm) thickness and line a greased 9" (23cm) pastry or pie dish. Chill for ten minutes.

Purée the pumpkin by peeling it, cubing it 1" (2.5cm) by 1" (2.5cm) and cooking very gently for no more than 15 minutes in a little water until it is soft enough to blend in a liquidiser or processor. You can also steam the pumpkin wich is an excellent method as it prevents it becoming watery.

Combine all the spices, the sugar and the salt in a bowl and then mix in the puréed pumpkin. Add the beaten eggs and stir briskly until the mixture is smooth. Finally add the cream and pour into the flan case.

Preheat the oven 375°F/190°C/gas mark 5 and bake the pie for 40−45 minutes until a knife inserted into the centre comes out clean. Can be eaten hot or cold.

Calabaza Enmielda

Serves 6–8

2lb (900g) pumpkin
4 tablespoons water
4oz (110g) dark soft brown sugar
4 fl oz (100ml) Cornish clotted or thick
   Loseley cream

Peel the pumpkin, remove seeds and any strands of fibre. Chop into sections 2″ (5cm) wide and ½″ (1cm) thick. Lay the slices in a wide bottomed pan and add the water and the sugar. Bring the pan to the boil, then turn down the heat and simmer until the pieces are tender but not disintegrating.

Drain and serve with the cream.

Ricotta Cheese with Rum and Black Coffee

An Italian delicatessen is probably the best source for fresh ricotta. Ask if you may taste a piece to make sure that there is no stale edge to it as this dish will be ruined if the cheese is not absolutely fresh.

Serves 4

12oz (350g) ricotta cheese
2 fl oz (50ml) very strong Columbian coffee
4oz (110g) castor sugar
2 fl oz (50ml) dark Barbados rum (Mount Gay
  if possible)
1½oz (40g) walnuts, finely chopped, optional
½" (1cm) stick of cinnamon, ground, optional

Pass the cheese through a strainer. Beat the rum, coffee and sugar together until the sugar has dissolved and then gently mix this into the cheese. Leave it for 1 hour at room temperature.

Divide the mixture into individual bowls and refrigerate for a further hour.

Serve topped with the walnuts or cinnamon.

Rum Chestnut Dessert

Serves 2

16 châtaigne or chestnuts, skinned and peeled
1 tablespoon sugar
1 egg yolk
1 coffee cup strong black coffee (preferably
   dark roasted Honduran or Guatamalan)
1 tablespoon double cream
½ liqueur measure of rum

Put the châtaigne or chestnuts in a large flat bottomed pan and just cover with water. Add half the sugar and simmer until they are soft. Strain and set aside.

Take a double saucepan if you have one, (otherwise place a bowl over simmering water), and put in the egg yolk, the remaining sugar, the black coffee, cream and rum. Heat this mixture over a very low flame, stirring all the while, till it thickens. Pour this sauce over the chestnuts and chill.

A Rich and Moist Ginger Cake

Here is an excellent recipe for a dark cake, its very taste transports me back to the West Indies. As I write out the ingredients on this late afternoon on a whitish-grey January day, the exotic imagined aromas seem to be willing my winter-stifled senses back to life, while the Thames flows blackly in a lifeless tide below my garden wall.

4oz (110g) unsalted butter
4oz (110g) dark soft brown sugar
2 eggs
½lb (225g) plain flour
1 teaspoon ground ginger
10oz (275g) West Indian dark treacle (Fowlers)
2oz (50g) sultanas
2oz (50g) preserved ginger in syrup, finely
   diced
½ teaspoon bicarbonate of soda
2 tablespoons milk

Soften the butter and beat it to a cream then add the sugar and mix thoroughly. Beat in the eggs and fold in the flour and ground ginger into the mixture then add the treacle, sultanas and ginger. Stir the bicarbonate into the just warmed milk and mix all the ingredients together very thoroughly.

Grease a 6″ (15cm) diameter cake tin and pour in the cake mixture and bake in a preheated oven 350°F/180°C/gas mark 4 for one hour. Then reduce to approximately 300−325°F/150−170°C/gas mark 2−3 for another 40 minutes (or less if you prefer a very moist cake).

This cake is very good served warm with cream that has had dark rum worked gently into it.

Ginger Cake—Upside Down

This is a recipe that I found in the West Indies which never fails to work. The texture is wonderfully moist, reminding me of the delicious cakes that my husband's sister used to send to us. It is the black treacle in this recipe which gives the cake such a rich and tempting appearance.

For the topping:

3 mangoes (I use tinned pears when in
   England)
1½oz (40g) butter
2oz (50g) brown sugar
1 tablespoon honey

For the cake mixture:

6oz (175g) unsalted butter
6oz (175g) castor sugar
3 eggs, beaten
1 level dessertspoon black treacle
8oz (225g) plain flour
2 teaspoons baking powder
1 rounded teaspoon ground ginger
1 rounded teaspoon mixed spice

Skin the mangoes then slice off each cheek and lay the slices, (or the tinned pears, if you are not using mangoes), flat down in a 10" (21cm) greased baking tin. Melt the butter, sugar and honey together in a pan until they are all dissolved. Stir together and then pour over the mangoes without disturbing their symmetry in the tin.

Cream the butter and sugar until light, then add the beaten eggs and treacle. Mix together the dry ingredients and fold them into the cake mixture. Spoon over the mangoes. Bake in the oven at 350°F/170°C/gas mark 3 for 35 minutes or a little longer depending on the depth of the mixture. I used to cook this cake in a Spanish earthenware bowl which was about 10½" (25cm) and 1½" (3cm) deep and it cooked very well in 35 minutes.

Sorbet Pina Colada

Serves 4–6

16 fl oz (450ml) unsweetened pineapple juice
3½oz (100g) granulated sugar
7 fl oz (200ml) water
3 soupspoons dark rum
3½ fl oz (100ml) coconut milk
2 egg whites

Put the pineapple juice and sugar into a saucepan with the water. Heat gently until the sugar dissolves. Turn up the heat and quickly bring the syrup to the boil.

Take off the heat and straight away add the rum and coconut milk; mix it in gently. Allow to cool slightly and then pour into a bowl. Leave to set for about 1½ hours in the freezer, stirring it regularly until hard round the edges.

Whip the egg whites till firm and fold into the contents of the bowl. Place the mixture back in the freezer and allow the sorbet to set for about 24 hours, beating it every so often to eliminate any ice crystals. Leave for a further two hours without touching until very hard.

Crushed Ice Fruit Breakfast

The fruits of the tropics are quite exotic beyond belief and must be plucked and eaten there and then. In 1793 J. B. Moreton's journal gives an account of his experiences which, when read in this cooler, darker part of the globe, fills me with nostalgia and longing:

When the scorching toils of the day are over, I often escorted them (the ladies) along the lime or cane intervals and sometimes through thickets of Guinea Grass six or seven feet high, to pluck at star apples, neeseberries, oranges; and when the starry mantled night spread her sable canopy, and luna only guided our footsteps, we frequently went to the river where we all bathed naked together without restraint or formality.

This is a very simple breakfast dish and a wonderfully cooling way to start the day—in the tropics especially. Effort must be made to choose the fruit carefully in the market—be sure to examine the produce before buying. Blemishes will not only look poor in the dish but will also probably not last long enough to make it till the next morning.

pineapple
mango
paw paw (papaya)
banana
orange (if in the Caribbean the Jamaican
   Ortanique variety is superb)
lime
naseberry (known as kimets in Jamaica and
   Trinidad) or strawberry

Take a large glass bowl and fill it with ice which you have crushed by putting into a clean towel and then bashed against a wall. Keep in the fridge until the fruit has been prepared.

Cut the pineapple diagonally into eight sections. Cut again into sections ½" (1cm) apart. Leave on the skin.

Cut the mango down each side avoiding the stone, giving you two cheeks from each fruit. Do not peel but cut into two.

Do not peel the naseberry but cut into four sections like an apple. Remove the black pips.

Dissect the paw paw like the pineapple and remove the shiny black seeds.

Cut the oranges into four sections. Do not peel.

Cut the limes into four sections—the aroma from this fruit alone will be pungent enough to wake you up!

Leave the bananas till last as they will discolour rapidly. Using a stainless steel knife peel and chop the bananas.

Remove the bowl from the fridge and quickly arrange the fruit on top and serve. An accompaniment of Jamaica Blue Mountain Coffee served fresh and black with a liqueur glass of Appleton's Light Golden Rum makes an excellent start to a tropical holiday.

Punches and Coolers

Mrs. Carmichael, that stalwart traveller of the early eighteen hundreds, wrote, 'I was much struck at first by the quantities of liquid drunk by many in the forenoon, commonly water just tinged with rum, though by older settlers, syrup, water and tamarind beverage. Newcomers seldom relish these drinks. Those who have only been a year or two from Europe do not experience the intense thirst of those who have long been resident in the tropics.' She goes on to say, and I find myself nodding in agreement 'the constitution becomes more relaxed and the desire for liquid increases.' Ah, how many pleasant evenings come back to me.

Mrs. Carmichael was quite correct in observing that water was drunk tinged with rum. First time visitors to the islands naturally seek out the more exotic punches and coconut laced concoctions. However, those who have spent some time in the West Indies find that their tastes change and that they begin to demand only the clear evocative smell of the rum. The West Indies produces the best rum in the world and each island produces something different. The names of the various brands evoke something of the history—Captain Morgan, Gold Label, Trelawny, Appleton Estate, Cavalier. I would recommend trying one measure of dark rum, with a thin slice of lime, a little water and a piece of ice added. Sip very slowly. Much preferable to immediately swamping the rum with all the other exotic ingredients on offer.

Almost since the Spaniards first brought sugar to the West Indies in the 16th century, rum has been the national drink of its peoples. A drink for all occasions and all classes, it has become an integral part of the life and soul of the islands. From Haiti to Barbados, Puerto Rico to Martinique, each island has its own style of rum, ranging from the light rums of Cuba to the heavier and richer rums of Jamaica. An extraordinary account from the 18th century illustrates both the excesses of that age and also the central role that rum played in social events.

A marble basin, built in the middle of the garden especially for the occasion, served as a bowl. Into it were poured 1,200 bottles of rum, 1,200 bottles of Malaga wine, and 400 quarts of boiling water. Then 600 pounds of the best cane sugar and 200 powdered nutmegs were added. The juice of 2,600 lemons were squeezed into the liquor. Onto the surface was launched a handsome mahogany boat piloted by a boy of twelve, who rowed about a few moments, then coasted to the side and began to serve the assembled company of six hundred, which gradually drank up the ocean upon which he floated.

Rum is made either from cane juice or molasses, the residue left over after the juice has been boiled to make sugar. Distilled either in a pot still or a continuous still, rum nowadays is becoming more and more standardised as the large companies begin to squeeze out the smaller ones. However there are still many marvellous rums to be found on the island; rums that can be drunk on their own or used as the base for the punches that follow in this chapter.

In Grenada the heat would leave the sun around four-thirty in the afternoon and the sun would seemingly increase its speed of descent to the horizon and disappear into the sea like a great fireball, leaving the sea, sky and our veranda bathed in lights of violet and gold. Within minutes complete darkness would envelop the world. The trade winds caressed our skin, and the rum our minds and bodies into a delicious state of bliss and oneness with the world. The rhythmic song of the cricket and the sweet whistle of the frogs was music in our ears. At the end of every day of hard work this was always to be relied upon to be our reward.

Remember! All the recommended measures in the recipes that follow can be adjusted to suit personal preferences.

Clear Syrup

A regular habit in the West Indies is to have a bottle of ready prepared syrup in the refrigerator. Sugar does not easily dissolve in alcohol so the syrup is a great standby and very quick to use. Since it is already smoothly fused with water, I believe it also makes the drink more potent when alcohol is added.

4oz (110g) white sugar
1 pint (570ml) cold water

Place the sugar and water into a bottle. Shake from time to time until fully dissolved. Refrigerate and use when needed.

Fruit Syrup

It is interesting to note on reading Eliza Acton's recipe for pineapple syrup the interchange of ideas that was taking place in the eighteen hundreds between England and her colonies. The pineapple was brought here, the syrup went there.

Eliza Acton's recipe for pineapple syrup is of interest in that as well as using pineapple as a flavouring one could also substitute other fruit such as, mango, nutmeg fruit, papaya and the incredible hogs plum. At certain times of the year, when driving along the narrow country roads of Grenada, when the towering hog plum tree was shedding its fruit on to the road, our wheels would crush the fruit and release the most marvellous scent that would then waft in through the car windows. So heady was the aroma that we had to stop and gather as much fruit as we could carry. We would wash the plums and then squeeze them in a clean thin cloth, extracting all the juices. Then we would add it to rum along with a little sugar. To my mind it is, after the passion fruit, the best fruit juice of all. But you will never find it on sale in the islands!

Here is Eliza Acton's recipe for pineapple syrup:

After having pared away every morsel of the rind from a ripe and highly flavoured pineapple cut ¾ of a pound of the fruit into very thin slices and then dice. Pour into it nearly ½ pint of spring water, heat and boil gently until it is extremely tender, then strain and press the juice gently from it through a cloth or through a muslin strainer folded in four. Strain it clear, mix it with 10 oz of the finest sugar in small lumps and when it is dissolved boil the syrup gently for a quarter of an hour. It will be delicious in flavour and very bright in colour if well made. If put into a jar and stored with a paper tied over it will remain excellent for weeks.

Banana Punch

Serves 1

It is as well to buy very ripe bananas, though the flesh should show no sign of brown and still be a cream colour throughout.

½ banana
sugar to taste
4 fl oz (110ml) coconut milk
1 measure rum
¼ teaspoon nutmeg, grated

Blend the banana, sugar and coconut milk together, and then pour into a glass half filled with crushed ice. Add the rum and nutmeg and stir.

Coconut Milk Rum Punch

In Jamaica they serve a concoction of bottled Guinness, rum, evaporated milk and sugar as a rum nog. Eliza Acton has a recipe called Cambridge Milk Punch which is clearly a precursor of the Jamaican version.

'Throw into 2 quarts of new milk the very thinly pared rind of lemon and ½ pound of good sugar in lumps, bring it slowly to the boil, take out the lemon rind, draw it from the fire and stir quickly in a couple of well whisked eggs which have been mixed with less than ½ pint of cold milk and strained through a sieve. The milk must not be allowed to boil after these are mixed with it. Add gradually a pint of rum and ½ pint of brandy. Mix the punch to a froth and serve immediately with quite warm glasses.'

From the above recipe one can see what a marvellously exact writer Eliza Acton was, writing at a time when the moral England she knew was vanishing. As Elizabeth David says in her introduction to the recently revised *Modern Cookery (1845)*, born in 1799 'Eliza Acton was in taste and spirit a child of the eighteenth century' and her book 'the crystallization of pre-industrial England's taste in food and attitude to cookery.' I have introduced her into the book so frequently as she illustrates perfectly the very influences that were taken from England to the Caribbean.

My own present day version of Eliza Acton's recipe follows.

Serves 6–8

2 pints (1.1 litre) coconut milk
4oz (110g) sugar
2 egg yolks
¼ teaspoon lime, grated
dark rum to taste and preference
freshly grated nutmeg, optional

Blend a fresh coconut (see techniques on page 23). Pour the coconut milk, sugar, egg yolks and grated lime into a blender and whizz. Taste. Add a measure of dark rum to each glass and pour the liquid over—grated nutmeg makes an excellent addition if absolutely fresh. Evaporated milk may be substituted for the coconut milk and is still rather good.

In many bars in the Caribbean this drink is served in a fresh green coconut. Just slice the top off the coconut—drink the coconut water laced with a little rum to refresh yourself as you labour to produce the coconut punch. Blend all the ingredients including the rum together and pour into the coconut half and serve with a straw. It makes a wonderful unbreakable glass, especially if you drink it sitting in crystal clear emerald waters, gently rocking with the current. More difficult to imagine doing this on the edge of the English Channel—however, hot summer afternoons will make a tolerable substitute as you serve this punch to friends while you tell them how wonderful it really is in the right setting.

Rum and Coconut Milk

A surprisingly good substitute for coconut milk is evaporated milk with water added as instructed on the label.

Serves 1

1 measure dark rum
4 fl oz (110ml) coconut milk (page 23)
sugar to taste
nutmeg, freshly grated

Combine all the ingredients, except for the nutmeg, in a cocktail shaker. Pour into a tumbler three-quarters filled with ice. Grate nutmeg on the top.

Rum Punch

I well remember a journey, not lightly undertaken, in a local bus in Jamaica. High in the Blue Mountains darkness comes early and a chill I had not felt for months touched my skin. The bus took off lurching down the mountain side, horns blaring, with no intention of stopping for any oncoming vehicle, man or donkey. Occasionally the road would widen a little and we bounded past another lorry, the sides hung with tilley lamps flaring in the wind, dark faces peering between the slats. The timing was quite miraculous; how we didn't meet on some narrow precipitous stretch of the road I shall never know. The burnt sugar scent of the cane fields just cut, clung to the cold wind. Parties of men returning from the fields stood back from our on-rushing bus, their machetes glinting in the bright tropical moonlight. Gradually through the extraordinarily purified air, the glittering lights of Kingston appeared below us as we hurtled on and down towards the plains. Upon arriving back at our house, the first thing to do was to unwind with a large rum punch.

J. B. Moreton's account in the late seventeen hundreds of the liking for sweet, cool drinks adds a certain spice to the proceedings:

They are very fond of all kinds of sweetmeats and sweet liquors: cool drink or mauby (a fermented liquor, made of sugar, water and lignumvita) is a delicious nectar to them in the morning:— I often laughed heartily at hearing a creole master or miss say, 'Do, momma, get me some mauby, mine head no 'tand good'. It is quite usual for a creole gentleman after dinner to send to the field for one of his favourite wenches, who is instantly hurried home and conveyed to his chamber.

There is an old formula which is very popular in the West Indies. If you ask a barman what he puts in his punch he will quote you 'One of sour, two of sweet, three of strong, four of weak.' This can be a little maddening when you are served a really superb punch and want to reproduce it exactly at home. The following recipe fits perfectly into the old saying quoted above and is quite simply wonderful.

Serves 1

1 fl oz (25ml) freshly squeezed lime juice
2 fl oz (50ml) syrup (page 163)
3 fl oz (75ml) dark rum
4 fl oz (110ml) water
dash of Angostura bitters
nutmeg, freshly grated
cherry or slice of lime or orange, optional

Pour the first four ingredients over a few rocks of ice. Add a dash of Angostura bitters and a grating of nutmeg. Sometimes a red cherry or a slice of lime or orange (very thinly sliced) is added for exotic effect.

White Rum Punch

The following account from Mrs. Carmichael in 1833 of limes being crushed as cartwheels ride over them, even now, evokes such memories that I can almost smell the scent of the limes as I write, reminding me of a wonderfully powerful concoction. 'The road was grown over with grass and the deep ruts of the sugar carts' wheels rendered skilful driving absolutely necessary: many a juicy lime was crushed in driving up.' Such is the quantity of lime used in this that I firmly believe the concentration of vitamin C saves one from the dire consequences usually associated with such an infusion!

Serves 1

1 very good measure of white rum, preferably
   Clarks Court from Grenada
1 whole lime, cut into quarters and slightly
   squeezed
crushed ice

Fill the glass to two-thirds and add the white rum and lime quarters.

Mango Drink with Rum

Serves 1

flesh of ½ large mango
1 measure rum
1 teaspoon lime juice
sugar, to taste
1–2 drops Angostura bitters

Choose a very ripe and juicy mango. Peel and reserve the flesh. If you are unable to obtain fresh mango then an excellent substitute is canned mango pulp or juice, available from most Indian grocers. Blend all the ingredients at top speed. Serve in a tall glass full of ice.

You can substitute papaya for the mango. Choose a small very ripe fruit—the flesh should be well yellowed—peel off the skin and remove the black seeds. Continue as above.

A Cool Mango Drink

Serves 6–8

2oz (50g) sugar or to taste
15 fl oz (400ml) water
1 teaspoon orange rind
1lb (450g) ripe mango flesh
15 fl oz (400ml) orange juice
¼ pint (150ml) lime juice
crushed ice, enough to fill a long glass
dark rum, as desired

Combine the sugar, water and orange rind in a saucepan and heat, stirring until the sugar has dissolved. Leave to cool.

Press the mangoes through a sieve and add to the cooled syrup. Add the freshly squeezed orange and lime juice and chill in the fridge. Serve on crushed ice with or without rum.

All the quantities may of course be adjusted to suit your taste, especially the sugar and rum.

Sangaree

In 1602 the Dutch East India Company was formed and held the monopoly for trading in cloves and nutmegs. Spices were highly prized at this time and English cooking became laden with pepper, cloves, cinnamon, nutmeg, ginger and sugar. By the mid 1700s the British East India Company began to be a power to be reckoned with and English cooking turned in the direction we can recognise today. Sugar and spices became more readily available and cheaper. There was an increase in the variety of fruit and vegetables grown, and spices, no longer a much sought after commodity, began to be used with more discretion—although spiced drinks were still very fashionable in the country houses. Elizabeth David in her book *Spices, Salt and Aromatics* found a recipe of this sort from Sir Harry Lukes' *Tenth Muse*, his source being a traditional eighteenth century mid-morning or luncheon drink which is still served to this day at the Bridgetown Club:

1 sherry glass of Madeira, ½ pint water, lime, a pinch of nutmeg, sugar to taste. Squeeze the lime into the Madeira and water and add the remaining ingredients, shake well. Serve as a long drink.

For my taste I would improve it by filling the glass with crushed ice first and then adding a hint of Angostura bitters, thus bringing it into the twentieth century.

Bibliography

Ashton Court Collection. Bristol Council Archives.

Spring Plantation Papers. Bristol Council Archives.

Dorset Dishes of the Seventeenth Century. Steven Cox. Century.

Food in Antiquity. Don & Patricia Brothwell. Thames & Hudson.

The Wheels of Commerce. Collins.

Spices, Salt & Aromatics. Elizabeth David. Penguin.

The Discovery of Guiana. Ed. V. T. Harlow.

Six Months in the West Indies. Henry Nelson Coleridge.

The Voyage of Sir Robert Dudley (1899). Ed. G. F. Warner. Hakluyt Society.

Domestic Manners and Social Conditions of the White, Coloured and Negro Population of the West Indies. (1833). Mrs. Carmichael.

Travels in Trinidad (1803). P. F. MacCullum.

Colonising Expeditions to the West Indies and Guiana 1623–1667 (1925).

Voyages of Sir James Lancaster (1877). Sir James Lancaster. Hakluyt Society.

History of Trinidad (1838). E. L. Joseph.

Manners and Customs (1793). J. B. Moreton.

The Loss of Eldorado. V. S. Naipaul. André Deutsch.

Book of Household Management (1859). Mrs. Beeton. Ward Lock.

Modern Cookery (1845). Eliza Acton. Longman, Green, Longman.

Illustrations taken from

A Picturesque Tour of the Island of Jamaica (1825). James Hakewill.

Daguerian Excursions in Jamaica (1850). Adolphe Duperly.

Sketches of Character (1837). I. M. Belisario.

Views of Trinidad (1851). M. J. Cazabon.

West India Scenery. R. Bridgens.

Index